Most Valuable Player
and Four Other All-Star Plays
for Middle and High School Audiences

Smith and Kraus, Inc.

Plays, Monologues, and Scenes for Grades 7–12

Dramatics Magazine's Best Plays for High School

New Plays from A.C.T.'s Young Conservatory, Volume I

New Plays from A.C.T.'s Young Conservatory, Volume II

New Plays from A.C.T.'s Young Conservatory, Volume III

Tim Mason: Ten Plays from the Minneapolis Children's Theatre

Plays of America from American Folklore for Grades 7–12

Seattle Children's Theatre: 6 Plays for Young Audiences

Short Plays for Young Actors

Villeggiatura Trilogy, Condensed for Young Actors

Great Monologues for Young Actors, Volume I

Great Monologues for Young Actors, Volume II

Great Scenes for Young Actors, Volume I

Great Scenes for Young Actors, Volume II

Monologues & Scenes for Middle School Actors

Multicultural Monologues for Young Actors

Multicultural Scenes for Young Actors

The Smith and Kraus Play Index for Young Actors

If you require pre-publication information about upcoming Smith and Kraus books, you may receive our semi-annual catalogue, free of charge, by sending your name and address to *Smith and Kraus Catalogue, 4 Lower Mill Road, North Stratford, NH 03590.* Or call us at (800) 895-4331, fax (603) 922-3348. WWW.SmithKraus.Com.

Most Valuable Player

and Four Other All-Star Plays
for Middle and High School Audiences

By Mary Hall Surface

YOUNG ACTORS SERIES

SK
A Smith and Kraus Book

A Smith and Kraus Book
Published by Smith and Kraus, Inc. PO Box 127, Lyme, NH 03768

Copyright ©1999 by Mary Hall Surface
All rights reserved
Manufactured in the United States of America

First Edition: July 1999
10 9 8 7 6 5 4 3 2 1

Book design by Julia Hill Gignoux, Freedom Hill Design
Cover Photo © California Theatre Center

The Library of Congress Cataloging-In-Publication Data
Surface, Mary Hall.
Five Plays for Middle and High School Audiences / by Mary Hall Surface. —1st ed.
p. cm. — (Young actors series)
Contents: Most valuable player — Prodigy — Dancing Solo — Broken Rainbows — Blessings.
ISBN 1-57525-178-7
1. Children's plays, American. 2. Young adult drama, American. [1. Plays.] I. Title. II. Title: Five plays.
III. Series: Young actors series.
PS3569.U718F5   1999
812'.54—dc21   99-30018
CIP

CONTENTS

Preface by Joe Dowling   VII

Introduction by Graham Whitehead   IX

Most Valuable Player   1

Prodigy.   33

Dancing Solo   71

Broken Rainbows. 105

Blessings 133

PREFACE

The theater is a powerful and magical medium of communication. At its best, it is a transforming experience that helps us to understand ourselves, our emotional connections to other people, our relationships to different cultures and to our collective humanity. It survives in the age of instant global connections because the need that it fulfills is as basic and fundamental as life itself. Those who, in each generation, predict the end of theater because of advancing technology are consistently proved wrong by an art form that nourishes imaginations and answers profound questions about the world we live in. Theater is also a place of entertainment— a source of celebration that creates the communal joy of laughter and release.

What distinguishes Mary Hall Surface as a writer for young audiences is her instinctive grasp of what actually moves and inspires young imaginations. She writes with an authority that entertains but also challenges her audience to face the reality of their lives. In doing so, she gives a powerful theatrical voice to the hopes and dreams, fears and failures of contemporary young people. She also knows how theater works. Her skill as a director infuses the plays with the knowledge of a practitioner, as well as the inspiration of a writer. This makes these plays wonderful to produce.

I hope that this anthology inspires many new productions of these fine plays. American theaters need to fully embrace the next generation, not only for reasons of future marketing, but also to help enrich our diverse community by embracing the future shapers of our society. By opening the world of theater to this eager audience, by offering them a means of expressing themselves through art, we can help young people understand the confusing world that they will inherit.

Joe Dowling
Artistic Director
The Guthrie Theater
Minneapolis, Minnesota, 1999

INTRODUCTION

For almost two decades, Mary Hall Surface has been deeply committed to the creation of the very best theater for young audiences. In a busy life of writing and directing plays throughout North America, Japan, and Europe, in all her travels to address symposia and plead for the need for serious theater for young people, throughout all her experimentations with style, one very simple belief drives her forward:

> I am fighting for the dignity of the individual. I would like every young person in my audience to have a life that allows them to be cared for…and to have beauty in their life.

Interview, *Intelligencer Journal*
Lancaster Pa., Friday, February 26, 1988

The five plays in this collection reflect this passionate concern beautifully. Whether the setting is seventeenth-century Vienna or contemporary North America, whether the protagonist is a white female adolescent, a famous black baseball player or a long dead musical icon, all of the plays are inspired by this deeply held concern for the emotional, spiritual, and physical well-being of the audience to whom and for whom she speaks.

Mary Hall Surface and I found ourselves one year on a panel at the International Children's Festival in Vancouver, Canada. I was to speak passionately in favor of fairy tales. Mary Hall Surface spoke passionately for the importance of theatrical material that dealt with the immediate and harsh social realities that children face. We entitled our exchange "One Coin, Two Sides." It is an entertaining take on reality that Mary Hall Surface talked to me about writing this introduction while she was directing an adaptation of six Brothers Grimm fairy tales and I was armpit deep in the intricacy of a piece for children written from the point of view of a Holocaust survivor. Still the same coin, we'd just temporarily flipped sides.

The point here, apart from the realization that one's point of view changes, is that theater for young audiences should not be an exclusive proposition, but a mixed offering. Children need all the theatrical nourishment they can get, and they deserve the attention and the passionate commitment from the best writers, directors, and performers in the country. They need to be challenged and encouraged to challenge and question in their turn.

The present collection could be seen as coming from the "social" or "problem" side of the coin about which Mary Hall Surface and I debated so energetically those years ago. But none of these plays suffer from the didactic, overbearing educational flaws that make some plays dedicated to the well-being of young people such a gloomy chore to read or attend. Mary Hall's dedication to the art of writing for young audiences comes from a much richer source of inspiration than merely the need to deal with social problems. Her plays are clearly character-driven as much as they are issue-driven. While the thematic material is an essential part of each play's appeal, the rich theatricality of the pieces is an equally essential part of their interest and their challenge. Her work demands the imaginative interaction between audience and actor. Thus, in this collection, both sides of the theatrical coin are well served.

Thematically, a number of concerns link these five plays. All of them deal in one form or another with social issues— racism being the most obvious. But a number of more personal issues are worth noting. In every play it is very clear that personal choice is a fundamental driving concern of the playwright. For Mary Hall Surface, the ultimate responsibility for our lives rests in our own hands. Yes, she says, young people are faced with huge pressures, cruel indifference, even active, outrageous brutality. Yes, these often make life unfair. But no matter the circumstances, she insists, we must choose our lives. This is not to say that she is unsympathetic to the pressures that her characters are under. Indeed, she expresses emotional outrage over their difficulties. But to survive, still more to prosper, in the contemporary world, Mary Hall Surface believes that we must *know* that we have choices and that it is our right and our obligation to make them. The underlying mantra of the plays in this collection is: We must embrace the responsibility of making choices and living with the consequences.

In *Most Valuable Player, Dancing Solo,* and *Blessings* this pattern is clear. Each character in these largely optimistic plays undertakes, almost as a rite of passage, an acknowledgment of their responsibility for their lives. But in

Broken Rainbows we have, in the character of Joel, a distortion of this paradigm. Joel works hard in his recyling job to achieve the end result that he knows he is capable of and, in his own mind, entitled to. Damond is less committed to earnest endeavor and achieves his job success somewhat ambiguously. In Joel's mind, when Damond is awarded a coveted management internship, he is stealing an undeserved prize. The author is careful to present both sides impartially, but one thing is clear from this play. We must learn that life is not always fair. We don't always get what we work for. Nonetheless, we are still responsible for our lives. We cannot and must not abdicate that responsibility, because to do so is destructive. In *Broken Rainbows,* the shattered window and the final unwound, useless music tape are the physical manifestations of the collapse of the dreams brought on by Joel's actions—his use of racial epithets to express his pain. His destructive despair in the face of a disappointing reality in turn damages Gina, a purely innocent bystander, in the struggle between Jewish-American Joel and African-American Damond. To me, *Broken Rainbows* presents us with a richer and more profoundly personal message than the simple, while still important, one of racial tolerance and understanding. To that message, Mary Hall has annealed the truth of a more personalized morality. We have to carry the responsibilies of our lives and actions. Joel fails in his aspirations and gives up, destroying his own life and those connected to him.

Not only does Mary Hall Surface insist that, whatever the given circumstances and however great the difficulties, young people are still the final arbiters of their fate; she also shows clearly in this group of five plays that choices are achieved only by dedication, commitment, and struggle. There is no *deus ex machina* to help with a scholarship, no angel riding to the rescue, no prince releasing a sleeping princess with a magic kiss. Instead of the traditional happily-ever-after model, she presents us with a much more existential world view: With or without us, life goes on and we know we are alive because we struggle. Like Camus's *Stranger,* she demands we get our teeth into life just as life will surely get its teeth into us.

I think that this is one of the great appeals of these plays to their target audience of middle and high school students. These young people are much more likely to listen and respond to work that acknowledges the difficulties of life in the late twentieth century than they are to overly optimistic sugar-coated visions of a rose-colored new millenium. The very young need to believe that things will work out; the adolescent needs to hear what he or she already knows—that life can present us with hard choices and mean circumstances. But even if the world around us is to be seen as a threatening, if not downright dangerous, place, Mary Hall Suface would have us work for our future successes *in the face of* these difficulties. If we do, we have, at least, a better chance of a fulfilled life.

Thus, in *Most Valuable Player,* Jackie Robinson is driven by his inner desire, his courage, and his refusal to submit to the horrendous negatives of social prejudice to achieve his historic goal of breaking the color barrier in professional baseball. In *Blessings,* Rene's learning-disability demons have given her an undeserved social battle to fight, but she doesn't give up until she achieves a peace and pride of achievement. Similarly, in *Dancing Solo,* Kara struggles to find her artistic expression as a dancer in spite of the unpredictability and pain rising from her mother's alcoholism. But for all of these characters, the cost is high. Jackie Robinson faces loneliness and physical danger to reach his goal. Rene's anguish is extreme precisely because she struggles so fiercely to find her true voice. The same can be said of Kara and even Joel. In all these plays, the author seems to be saying that the price for success is high but worth paying. In *Prodigy,* the question is raised as to whether the cost can be *too* high. Written during the time when Mary Hall Suface was living in California's Silicon Valley, that epicenter of high achievers, the play pleads for the right of children to be children.

Mozart, of all the leading characters in the five plays, achieves the greatest glory. His place in the pantheon of the greatest artists to ever have lived is secure forever, but at what cost? In *Prodigy,* Mary Hall Suface takes us first through the early joyful years when the Mozarts were a family who played both games and instruments together. But then she brings us to the point where Mozart has become a prisoner of his own genius, trapped by success, while the warmth and joy of a natural and healthy childhood is left aside. "You must be perfect," says Leopold, "for your music." But perfection is an inhuman achievement that demands crippling sacrifices. There are limits then, Mary Hall Suface is saying, to the price we allow ourselves or encourage our children to pay for success. The passion and the responsibility we must claim for our lives must be balanced. Not for nothing did Suface give another of her plays, one inspired by the work of mobile artist Alexander Calder, the approving title of *A Perfect Balance.* The golden mean is given a very modern context in her plays.

In these five plays, as well as in her other original and adapted plays, Mary Hall Suface is a fierce and practical advocate for our children's right to a freely chosen and holistic life. Her plays do reflect a credo that she wishes to foster, but she is an *artist* and not (despite, or perhaps because of, her familiarity with her father's duties as an Episcopal minister) a preacher. Her plays are designed for practical presentation, both by professional groups such as California Theatre Center (which was the original producing company of two of the present collection), and by schools and college groups. The cast size is small. The settings are indicated rather that heavily realistic. *Blessings* is the only possible exception to this rule with its realistic settings in and outside a mountain cabin. But generally the author invites, indeed demands, the creative and imaginative participation of her audience to help create the environment of the plays. In *Dancing Solo* ballet bars become not just the reality of the dance studio, but the school, the house, and, metaphorically, the prison of the soul with which Kara is threatened. *Most Valuable Player* relies on a backstop fence, benches, and a table top to create the entire environment of Jackie Robinson's life. The world of Mozart in *Prodigy* is created with mime and movement, puppet and mask, while *Broken Rainbows* relies on the physical skills of the actors to create not only mood, but also the setting of basketball courts and recycling trucks as well.

In all five plays, Mary Hall Surface demands much of her actors. They must frequently use more expressive outlets than merely the ability to use text. *Prodigy*, with its preoccupation with Mozart's musical career, is the most obvious example of integrating word with music. The text of the play is divided by the technical notation of a musical score. Indeed, the author has explained that stylistically she has always considered the play "a piece of music." Three of the other plays share a stylistic reliance on multiple art forms. In *Dancing Solo,* the whole play is built both on the metaphorical power and the actual physical beauty of dance. In *Broken Rainbows,* music again is both the bridge that links Gina and Joel, and the medium through which Gina can express her longing for a world "on the other side of now." In *Blessings,* the over-achieving Katie's music and Rene's painting give the girls a place to struggle with their deepest feelings. The poetry of Rene and of the gentle, introverted Jesse serves the same function. Jesse's struggle to read those words of the poem in the closing seconds of *Blessings* is for me one of the richest and most powerful moments in the whole collection—a moment in which metaphor and the reality of life's struggle are brilliantly fused.

So the actors, as well as the director, of a Surface play need to bring a rich and rounded artistic skill to bear on the work, as well as a sensitive ear for dialogue. Mary Hall Surface, for the most part, writes with a simple unadorned style. Even *Prodigy*, with its delicate evocation of a historically distant speaking style, remains comfortable for a modern ear. That the plays are still rich and theatrically powerful is because of the blend of straight-forward dialogue with the poetry of music and dance and painting. As Mary Hall Surface has said in a newspaper interview in 1994:

> I'm interested in beauty. In our culture...creating something beautiful with artistic integrity for young people...that is itself revolutionary.

Thus Mary Hall Surface struggles to achieve the same perfect balance of form and content in her own work that she sees in the mobiles of Alexander Calder. She seeks to achieve this artistic satisfaction through a synergy of message and medium. Whatever the medium, however, she believes above all that, "Theater must have something to say." Let me give her, as I am sure I tried not to do in Vancouver so many years ago, the last word:

> As theater artists we can address the issues that arise from the multicultural aspect of our communities and nations—imaginatively, confrontationally, metaphorically, realistically—whatever your artistic choice may be. But theater must strive to be a reflection of the society, or at least the *aspirations* of the society to which it belongs.

From Keynote Speech given at
ASSITEJ International Congress
Adelaide, Australia, April 1987

Graham Whitehead
Director and Playwright
Tempe, Arizona, 1999

Most Valuable Player

*Kevin Reese as Enos Blackwell and Dorien Wilson as Jackie Robinson
in* Most Valuable Player, *California Theatre Center, 1985.
Photo by California Theatre Center.*

ORIGINAL PRODUCTION

Most Valuable Player was conceived by Gayle Cornelison. It was written by Mary Hall Surface, with Charles Abernathy, Joseph Bostick, Gayle Cornelison, Duncan W. Graham, Helen Pettit, Kevin Reese, J. Steven White, and Dorien Wilson. It was directed by J. Steven White. The set design was by Paul Vallerga, costume design by Colleen Troy Lewis, and sound and slide design by Kevin Reese. The stage manager was Duncan Graham. It opened in Sunnyvale, California, in a middle-school gymnasium in May, 1984. The cast was as follows:

JACKIE ROBINSON	Dorien Wilson
BRANCH RICKEY	Chuck Abernathy
CHUCKIE	Chuck Abernathy
LEO DUROCHER	Kevin Reese
ENOS BLACKWELL	Kevin Reese
KEVIN	Kevin Reese
AL CAMPANIS	Kevin Reese
PEE WEE REESE	Joe Bostick
JOE	Joe Bostick
CLAY HOPPER	Joe Bostick
LARRY MCPHAIL	Joe Bostick
TRACK-TIMEKEEPER	Joe Bostick
RUTH WARTON	Helen Pettit
PHYLLIS HUNT	Helen Pettit
HELEN	Helen Pettit
COUNTRY WAITRESS	Helen Pettit
FRENCH CANADIAN WAITRESS	Helen Pettit

VOICE-OVERS: RADIO, MAC, MOMMA, RAE, ANNOUNCERS

NOTES FOR *MOST VALUABLE PLAYER*

Most Valuable Player was developed collectively by the California TheatreCenter in May 1984. The strength of the piece lies in the opportunities for versatile performers and simple, but imaginative staging. Each scene should flow rapidly into the next, relying upon sound and light to achieve transitions in place and time, rather than elaborate shifts of scenery. An absolute minimal use of props is strongly recommended. The performer's challenge is to create a number of characters, aided only by simple changes of costume pieces, often only from one baseball cap to another.

The original set for *Most Valuable Player* consisted of a backstop baseball fence unit, built of P.V.C. pipe, wire, and wood. The backstop was made of rear projection material. Four benches and a table top were reconfigured to create all environments. The sound tape is crucial to the production. Crowd sounds are critical to evoking the environment of the baseball park. The projections, seen throughout on the back of the set, should be designed from historical photographs of the period. Slides from the original production can be rented from the California Theatre Center or from the author.

The theatrical convention of the baseball sequences used both fast and slow motion in the original production. For example, the players might shift into slow motion once the pitcher begins his wind up, or when the batter hits the ball. It is also suggested that the position of home plate be varied in the different baseball sequences, so that the positions of the performers can highlight and give variety to each sequence.

Most Valuable Player has been presented to audiences of children and adults throughout the world. The production has been featured in a one-week residency at the Kennedy Center in Washington, D.C.; at the Edmonton, Toronto. and Vancouver International Children's Theatre Festivals; on a one-month tour of Canada sponsored by the Canada Council; on a fifty-two-day tour of Europe sponsored by the United States Government; and as the only American company at an International Theatre Festival in Lima, Peru. The strength of Jackie Robinson's character and his courage crosses boundaries of age, race, and nationality. We wish all producers much success with what has been an important and moving production for our company.

Mary Hall Surface
California Theatre Center, 1985

Most Valuable Player only became a reality because a number of dedicated artists made it possible. I would like to thank our director, J. Steven White for giving his time and talent, and I thank the American Conservatory Theater and its leader at the time, William Ball, for allowing Mr. White the time to devote to this project. Every member of our company in our 1983–84 season gave support to this project and their help will always be appreciated. Finally, the highest praise is due to every artist who worked directly on this production for the full rehearsal period. Their wonderful work made the success of the project possible, and without the work of every individual the final product would have been greatly diminished.

Gayle Cornelison
General Director
California Theatre Center, 1985

Since 1984, *Most Valuable Player* has been a part of my professional life like no other play on which I have had the privilege to work. After serving as the playwright for the collective process of the play's development, I had the opportunity to direct its many remounts for the California Theatre Center, and then to direct my own production at the Kennedy Center in Washington in 1989. I have been an artist-in-residence at many theaters and universities throughout the United States, helping more and more theaters bring *MVP* to their audiences. My greatest adventure with the play was directing it for Theatre Seigei, a professional theater for young audiences in Tokyo. Now thousands of middle-school students in Japan have shared Jackie's story. This play has a remarkable life, and I am thankful for having been a part of its beginning.

Mary Hall Surface
1998

LIGHTS UP slowly on JACKIE, circling the field.

RADIO: *(Voice-over.)* Good evening, folks. Mel Allen's sports corner. Dateline: September 15, 1948. The baseball season has come to a close and the Brooklyn Dodgers are once more the Brooklyn Bums. 1947's league champions have this year finished a disappointing third. And their hotshot second baseman, Jackie Robinson, last year's Rookie of the Year, is in my opinion, this year's biggest Bum. Final score of today's game: Giants 7, Dodgers nothin'…Giants 7, Dodgers nothin'…

JACKIE: *(He finally slows down. He stops.)* Giants 7, Dodgers nothin'. I let 'em down. I let 'em down! Mack! Can you hear me? Are you listening? Had I just come in this season and given it my all…if I had trained a little harder, it might have made the difference. I've let you down. I let Momma down…and Rachel…and our people, man. But I'm not gonna give up. No sir'ee. And you know why? Cause I'm a Robinson and Robinsons don't give up.

DUROCHER: *(Entering, as if in JACKIE's memory.)* Robinson, you're fat.

JACKIE: I just gained a few pounds.

DUROCHER: A few pounds? What'd you do during the off-season? Eat Philadelphia?

PEE WEE: *(Entering, as if in JACKIE's memory.)* Good God Almighty. What're you so upset about, buddy?

JACKIE: Ah, Pee Wee. I let the team down this season.

PEE WEE: Come on, Jackie. We're all pulling on the same wagon here—

JACKIE and PEE WEE: And you're our main horse.

PEE WEE: I mean it. You're the best pivot man in the major leagues. Don't you let anybody tell you any different.

RICKEY: *(Entering, as if in JACKIE's memory.)* Jackie—

JACKIE: Mr. Rickey.

RICKEY Do you know why you are here?

JACKIE: Why *am* I here?

RICKEY: Because you are a terrific ballplayer. I hired you, not because you are black, or because I had to, but because with you the Dodgers will win pennant after pennant. We'll win next year.

JACKIE: I'm sorry, Mr. Rickey. I'll make it up to you. Next year, I'll—

RICKEY: Jackie, don't take it so hard. Here, give me your hand. Jackie—

DUROCHER: Robinson!

RICKEY: Jackie!

DUROCHER: Robinson!

(The following lines of DUROCHER, PEE WEE, and MR. RICKEY overlap.)

DUROCHER: Your mistake is to think that I'm gonna manage a ballplayer who comes in at the top of spring training camp looking like a sausage!

PEE WEE: Come on, Jackie. We're all pulling on the same wagon here and you're our main horse. I mean it. You're the best pivot man in the major league. Don't you let anyone tell you any different.

RICKEY: Jackie, I hired you not because you are black or because I had to, but because with you the Dodgers will win pennant after pennant—

JACKIE: *(Yelling and breaking away.)* I let them down!!

(JACKIE and DUROCHER exit. LIGHTS transition to MR. RICKEY's office.)

RICKEY: It's a little late for you to be here, isn't it, Harold?

PEE WEE: Sorry to bother you, sir, but I'm a little concerned about Jackie. I'm afraid he's taken our final loss today and our third place finish a little hard. A few of us were havin' a couple of beers in the clubhouse after the game and Jackie just got up and left. I went out to check on him and there he was, just runnin' around the field.

RICKEY: *(Looking out window.)* Like that?

PEE WEE: *(Looking out window.)* Still down there.

RICKEY: What's wrong with him, Harold?

PEE WEE: Well, him comin' in at the beginning of the season overweight and all was tough on him. I figure he feels it's his fault for us not winning this year. It might help if you were to talk at him.

RICKEY: I'll do what I can, Harold.

PEE WEE: Thank you, sir.

(A knock at the door.)

RICKEY: Who's there?

RUTH: Ruth Warton.

PEE WEE: You want me to leave, sir?

RICKEY: Oh, Miss Warton, I forgot! Oh my gosh…let her in, Harold.

(PEE WEE opens the door.)

RICKEY: Miss Warton, I am so sorry—

RUTH: How do you do, Mr. Rickey. Thank you ever so much for arranging the tickets for today's game. I find this American baseball terribly exciting.

RICKEY: Harold, this is Ruth Warton of the *London Times*.

PEE WEE: Howdy Ma'am.

RICKEY: Miss Warton, this is Harold "Pee Wee" Reese, Captain of the Dodgers.

RUTH: Pee Wee Reese. Now let me see. You played the backstop.

PEE WEE: *Short*stop, Ma'am.

RUTH: Oh, right. Shortstop. How silly of me. Mr. Rickey, I am terribly interested in doing a story for the *London Times* on your Negro player, Jackie Robinson.

RICKEY: I don't think that will be possible, Miss Warton. *(Trying to get PEE WEE to join in his untruth.)* Hasn't Jackie gone home to California, Harold?

PEE WEE: I don't know, sir. I think so.

(Knock on the door.)

RICKEY: Who's there?

DUROCHER: *(Letting himself in.)* It's me, ya bum! Ya gonna ask me in?

RICKEY: Durocher!

DUROCHER: Hey, Mr. Rickey. It's good to see ya.

RICKEY: Mr. Durocher, this is Ruth Warton of the *London Times*. Miss Warton, this is Leo Durocher, our former manager.

DUROCHER: Currently manager of the New York Giants—the team that's been whipping the pants off the Dodgers all season long. Hey, Pee Wee, how ya been?

PEE WEE: Howdy, Leo.

DUROCHER: You guys have looked pretty slow against the Giants.

PEE WEE: Yeah, well, we tried our best.

DUROCHER: *(Looking out the window.)* Hey, Rickey, ya still got a player out on the field.

RICKEY: Leo—

DUROCHER: Wait a minute—that's Robinson!!

RICKEY: Leo!

DUROCHER: Hey, Mr. Sausage! This is the butcher talkin' to ya! Ah, he can't hear me—

PEE WEE: Come on, Leo. Let's go down to the clubhouse. I got a cold one with your name on it.

DUROCHER: Yeah, I'm comin'—

(DUROCHER and PEE WEE exit.)

RUTH: *(Pointedly.)* Gone home?

RICKEY: It seems I owe you an apology. Mr. Robinson has taken the Dodger's shortcomings this season rather personally. I don't think he'd give you much of an interview. I would be glad to help you in any way I can. Would you join me for dinner?

RUTH: Lovely. Thank you.

RICKEY: Let's see. Jack's family comes from Georgia. His grandfather was a slave, you know.

RUTH: A slave! Really?

(RUTH and RICKEY exit.)

RICKEY: *(Voice-over.)* And his father was only a little better off—a share-cropper. But his father abandoned the family when Jackie was just a baby. So, Jackie's mother took her five children and moved to Pasadena, California. It wasn't easy for Jackie growing up. His was the only Negro family in the neighborhood.

(During the voice-over young JACKIE and the children have taken apart the office and set the stage as a ball field. The kids move into place with CHUCKIE at bat, JOE pitching, and KEVIN and HELEN in the field. JACKIE watches from the side.)

KEVIN: OK, Chuckie, you're up.

JOE: It's gonna come right to you, Chuckie.

KEVIN: Choke up on the bat a little. There you go.

JOE: Here it comes.

(CHUCKIE swings and falls.)

KEVIN: You all right?

JOE: Come on, Chuckie, try again.

HELEN: You'll get it this time, Chuckie. Nice and slow there, Joe.

JOE: I'm pitchin' it as slow as I can.

JACKIE: *(Moving in closer.)* All right! A game!

ALL: OK, Chuckie. Here it comes. Keep your eye on the ball—

(CHUCKIE manages to hit the ball, he runs and is tagged out at second.)

JACKIE: *(Stepping into batter's box.)* You're outta there.

(All focus on JACKIE. HELEN marches to him, grabs the bat, and pushes him away.)

HELEN: Get outta here! Come on, who's pitchin'? Come on!!

JOE: Here we go.

(KEVIN pulls JACKIE onto the field. HELEN hits the ball but JACKIE makes a great catch.)

JACKIE: You're out, Babe Ruth.

HELEN: That does not count.

JACKIE: What do you mean?

HELEN: It doesn't count. We didn't ask you to play.

JOE: Yeah, get outta here.

JACKIE: You're just sore 'cause I got you out.

KEVIN: He lives in the neighborhood. Let him play.

HELEN: I know he lives in the neighborhood. But we don't want your kind here. 'Cause you're dirty.

JACKIE: I'm not dirty.

HELEN: That's what you are. Your houses are dirty. Your sidewalks are dirty. You're nothing but a dirty nigger!

JOE: Nigger!

CHUCKIE: Nigger!

HELEN: Dirty nigger!

JACKIE: Yeah! Well, you're a cracker!

HELEN: Soda cracker good to eat. Niggers only good to beat.

(HELEN throws the baseball at JACKIE. The others throw rocks at him. The following lines overlap as the kids run out.)

HELEN: You get back to Africa, little black sambo. Get outta here.

KEVIN: Dad! Dad!

JACKIE: Stop it! Stop it! *(JACKIE is now alone, on his knees, crying. He is isolated in light.)* Mack, Mack?!!

MACK: *(Voice-over.)* I'm here. I'm listenin'. What's the matter, little brother?

JACKIE: They hurt me. They hurt me real bad. All I wanted to do was play baseball with them. They threw rocks at me and called me names.

MACK: *(Voice-over.)* Names? What'd they say?

JACKIE: They called me nigger. Dirty nigger. Why'd they have to call me that?

MACK: *(Voice-over.)* Because they're stupid. Don't let them get to you. 'Cause if you want to play, you're gonna hear it all the time. Get your head up. Come on, stand up. Hey, you're a Robinson. And Robinsons don't give up.

JACKIE: Just like Momma says.

(JACKIE runs into his house and turns on the radio. [The specific environments are created by JACKIE through mimed actions. Each sequence should flow easily into the next.])

MOMMA: *(Voice-over.)* Jackie! Jack! Jackie Roosevelt Robinson! Don't let me have to call you no more, boy. Get your coat. You're gonna make us late for church.

RADIO: *(Voice-over.)*...going into the bottom of the 7th inning of the 1932 All-Star game. It's a perfect day for baseball. The National League is winning four to one...

JACKIE: *(Speaking over the radio.)* But Momma, the game's almost over.

MOMMA: *(Voice-over.)* What did I tell you about listenin' to them games all the time.

(The radio shuts off.)

MOMMA: *(Voice-over.)* That's a white man's game. They don't let colored folks play that game. Boy, you could be readin' and learnin' so when you get older, you can be somebody. Like a fine doctor.

JACKIE: I will be somebody, Momma. I wanna play ball. I'm a good player and I can do it.

MOMMA: *(Voice-over.)* Son, you can't play games all your life.

JACKIE: Mack's doin' it.

(JACKIE's house, four years later. Change of time need be suggested only by JACKIE turning his baseball cap forward, having worn it to the back in the earlier childhood sequences.)

RADIO: *(Voice-over.)* This is Mike Parker in Berlin at the 1936 Olympic Games. The finals for the 200 meter dash are about to begin. *(BANG.)* There's the gun! It's Jesse Owens out in front with an early lead. But here comes Mack Robinson hard and fast on the outside. He's moving into second place. It's Owens and Robinson. Owens and Robinson! And at the ribbon, it's the USA winning the gold and silver medals. Jesse Owens and Mack Robinson, these two great Negro athletes have taken first and second in the 200 meter dash.

JACKIE: You hear that, Momma?

RADIO: *(Voice-over.)* All hundred and ten thousand fans are on their feet. What? Adolph Hitler is leaving the stands. He's refusing to acknowledge these fine, black athletes—

JACKIE: *(Turning off the radio.)* He did it, Momma. I'm gonna do it, too. I'm goin' to the top!

MOMMA: *(Voice-over.)* I know you are, son. Go to the top. Go to college. Will you promise me that, son?

JACKIE: Momma, we don't have enough money. I want to get a job so I can get you outta scrubbin' white folks' floors.

MOMMA: *(Voice-over.)* I'll scrub floors for the rest of my life to give you a chance. It's a white man's world and you've got to have an education to make your way.

JACKIE: All right, Momma. I'll do it. I'll go to college.

(With the announcer voice-over, scene changes to college basketball court. NUMBER 25 rushes onto the court to meet JACKIE.)

ANNOUNCER: *(Voice-over.)* Driving down the court, Jackie Robinson, star forward of Pasadena City College, is—whoa! Intentional foul on Number 25! It'll be a one and one situation at the free-throw line. Robinson is stepping up to the line.

JACKIE: *(To NUMBER 25.)* Why don't you stick to the game?

NUMBER 25: Why don't you shut your black face, nigger.

JACKIE: *(Handing him the ball.)* You wanna hold this?

NUMBER 25: Sure.

(JACKIE decks him and proudly raises his hand when the foul whistle blows. JACKIE's attention is quickly diverted when he sees RAE [offstage] for the first time, which changes the scene.)

JACKIE: Hey, there. My name is Jackie Robinson. I'm a junior at UCLA.

RAE: *(Voice-over.)* I know.

JACKIE: I've got a ticket to tomorrow's meet. Wanna go?

RAE: *(Voice-over.)* Sure.

(TIMEKEEPERS, PHYLLIS, and JED, enter and set up track finish line. JACKIE prepares for the race and runs in slow motion during the announcer's speech.)

ANNOUNCER: *(Voice-over.)* On block number 7, the favorite for this race, Jackie Robinson of UCLA. This completes the field of the 100 yard dash at the NCAA National Track finals. Phyllis Hunt, official timekeeper, raises the gun. The runners are on their mark. They're set. *(BANG.)* They're off! Robinson takes an early lead. He's burning up the track. This has got to be a record time! At the ribbon—Robinson easily takes the race.

PHYLLIS: Official time—10 seconds flat.

ANNOUNCER: *(Voice-over.)* What? The official time is a disappointing 10 flat.

JACKIE: What do you mean? I know I was faster than that!

PHYLLIS: Can't argue with the clock, Robinson.

JACKIE: It must be wrong.

PHYLLIS: I guess you just didn't run as fast, boy.

JACKIE: *(He grabs the stopwatch from her, and throws it angrily.)* It's not right! Not fair!

PHYLLIS: You'll hear about this, Robinson! *(She exits, angrily.)*

JED: Hey Robinson. I think she might have started her watch early. I got 9.4. *(He exits.)*

JACKIE: 9.4. Well, all right! You hear that, Mack! I broke your record, man. And I'm gonna keep on breakin' records.

MACK: *(Voice-over.)* That's good little brother. Cause you're gonna have to run for the both of us now. The doctor says I can't run anymore. My heart won't take it. You're the winner now. Go straight to the top.

JACKIE: I'm goin' to the top. I'm gonna quit college. I'm gonna play pro-ball. Gonna make me some money.

RAE: *(Voice-over.)* You can't make any money playing pro-ball in a Negro league. You gotta finish college. How we gonna get married if you can't earn us a decent living?

JACKIE: Rae, honey, no amount of education is gonna make any difference for a black man. I'm gonna go and *make* the difference.

(RAE exits. RICKEY and RUTH re-enter. The interview continues.)

RICKEY: World War II came and Jackie joined the army. He was discharged from the service, honorably I might add! He refused to sit in the back of an army transport bus. Well, when he got back, he took a low-paying job while playing for the Monarchs—a semi-professional black baseball team in Kansas City.

(JACKIE mimes batting with the sound of honky-tonk music and an enthusiastic crowd in the background. JACKIE swings to great cheers.)

RICKEY: That was 1945. I believed that the time was right to convince the owners that we could no longer bar Negro players from the major leagues. Of course, they disagreed. Larry McPhail of the Yankees objected the loudest.

(JACKIE exits and MCPHAIL enters and addresses the audience as if at an owner's meeting.)

MCPHAIL: This has nothing to do with racial discrimination. It's all plain and simple dollars and cents. The Negro leagues will lose their best players so they'll fold. The Negro ball club owners will lose their investments. And think of the money we will lose when there are no Negro leagues to rent our stadiums to. That's why I say keep the Negroes in their own league. But let's hear what the players have to say. Enos Blackwell, St. Louis Cardinals.

ENOS: Gentlemen. Is nothing sacred anymore? Baseball is a white man's game. Always has been and always will be. To think of a white man and a nigg— *(Catching himself.)* Negro playin' on the same field…why, it's unthinkable. It's un-American. OK, Mr. Rickey, you can have your say.

RICKEY: Gentlemen, this country has just suffered through a war in which millions of young men gave their lives in defense of democracy. But it was not just white boys who died. Negro men fought alongside our sons like brothers. Now, would you have me believe that the Negro who was good enough to stop a bullet in his country's defense is not good enough to catch a baseball in the land he has defended? No! I cannot believe that! The greatest source of untapped talent in this country today is the Negro race. I am thoroughly convinced of the talent of ballplayers in the Negro leagues—players good enough for the major leagues. And one more thing—I have just gotten the OK from Commissioner Chandler and from my owners to proceed with the search for the right man. Nothing can prevent this, gentlemen. I suggest you'd best get used to the idea. Good day. *(RICKEY turns triumphantly and BLACKWELL and MCPHAIL exit in a huff. RUTH exits. Transition into RICKEY's office.)*

RICKEY: How do you do, Mr. Robinson. I've been looking forward to meeting you.

JACKIE: I've wanted to meet you, too, sir.

RICKEY: Welcome to Brooklyn.

JACKIE: Thank you, sir.

RICKEY: Now, Mr. Robinson. I'm going to get right to the point. Do you have a girl?

JACKIE: I beg your pardon, sir?

RICKEY: Do you have a girl? A girlfriend?

JACKIE: Uh, I'm not sure, sir.

RICKEY: Either you have a girl or you don't. Which is it, Robinson?

JACKIE: Well, you see, Mr. Rickey, I've been on the road with the Monarchs most of this year and I haven't been writing like I should. I like to think I have a girl, sir.

RICKEY: Good. Sit down, Jackie.

JACKIE: Thank you, sir.

RICKEY: How's your game?

JACKIE: Good. My game's real strong.

RICKEY: No problems?

JACKIE: I did have a shoulder injury but I'm fine now.

RICKEY: *(Placing a firm hand on JACKIE's shoulder.)* This shoulder?

JACKIE: *(Wincing just a little.)* Yes, sir.

RICKEY: Jackie, do you know why you are here?

JACKIE: Your scout told me that you're starting a Negro team to play at Ebbets Field—the Brown Dodgers.

RICKEY: Yes. That's what I told him to tell you. Now Jackie, I hear that at UCLA you were a racial agitator.

JACKIE: That's not true, sir. I was just standing up for what I thought was right.

RICKEY: Based on my research on you, Mr. Robinson, I think I would have to agree with you.

JACKIE: If I'd been a white player, they would have called me a competitor. But since it was me, they called me an agitator.

RICKEY: What do you think when they call you nigger?

JACKIE: I don't know, sir.

RICKEY: Come on, Jackie, what do you do?

JACKIE: I fight back, sir.

RICKEY: With your fists? Or with your hitting, your running, and your fielding?

JACKIE: Look, Mr. Rickey, I don't understand. What difference does it make if I'm gonna be playing with an all-Negro team?

RICKEY: I'm afraid I've led you on, Jackie. There are no Brown Dodgers. *(Pause.)* You have been scouted to play for the Brooklyn Dodgers.

JACKIE: Me?

RICKEY: Yes, Mr. Robinson.

JACKIE: But I'm black, sir.

RICKEY: I realize that. I just hope that you are the *right* black man to make this work. Do you have the courage to take what they will throw at you? To play hard, but clean?

JACKIE: If you know anything about me, sir, you know I've got guts.

RICKEY: What you are in for takes a different kind of guts. Let me give you an example: now, you're playing second—come on, is that the way you play second base?

(RICKEY has taken off his coat to act out each example and expects JACKIE to do the same. JACKIE joins in.)

RICKEY: Good! Now, I'm that man on first and I want to win—*bad!* When I run to second, I do this.

(Knocks JACKIE down.)

RICKEY: And knock you flat and say, "How do you like that, nigger boy?" Come on.

(He pulls JACKIE to his feet.)

RICKEY: You're at a restaurant. You've just gotten off the team bus. You're hot. Hungry. And I'm behind the counter and I say to you, "We don't serve niggers here."

JACKIE: That's OK. I don't eat niggers.

RICKEY: Now, that's just the kind of answer that will get you into trouble. All right. Back on second.

(RICKEY and JACKIE are acting out each step.)

RICKEY: Now, it's the last game in the World Series. It's hot. Ebbets Field is like a frying pan and you're in the middle of it. I'm on first and pow! The ball is coming right at you and so am I. I spike you! The blood is running down your leg, but you don't budge an inch because you're a heck of a ballplayer. I feel your glove in my ribs and I know I'm out. I look up at you and all I see is your face—that sweaty, stinkin' black face—and I punch you right in the cheek. What do you do?

JACKIE: I turn the other cheek. That's what you want me to say, isn't it? Look, Mr. Rickey, if you want me to cringe every time some white man says "boo" you've got the wrong man. I take plenty, Mr. Rickey, but I won't let any man run all over me.

RICKEY: You strike back, they'll throw you out of the game.

JACKIE: I'll always have the guts to fight back.

RICKEY: I want you to have the guts *not* to fight back! Don't you see, Jackie? You have the chance to rise above the pettiness, the brutality, and the stupidity that separates black from white. *(Pause.)* Are you a Christian, Jackie?

JACKIE: Yes, sir. I went to church every Sunday as a boy. My Momma made sure of that.

RICKEY: *(Handing him a small book, Papini's* Life of Christ.*)* Here, read this aloud.

JACKIE: "But, I say unto you, to answer blow with blow, evil deed with evil deed, is to meet the attacker on his own ground, to proclaim oneself as low as he. Only he who has conquered himself can conquer his enemies." *(Pause.)* I understand.

RICKEY: Can you conquer the enemy of prejudice, not with harshness, but with the strength of your spirit?

JACKIE: I can, sir, if you'll give me the opportunity.

RICKEY: It's yours, Jackie. Welcome to the Dodgers.

JACKIE: Thank you. Thank you, sir.

RICKEY: We'll be starting you with our farm team, the Montreal Royals, at $600 a month with a $3500 bonus. I want you to know that I am not going to treat you any differently than anyone else, except for one thing— I will always be there for you. I'll support you all the way. We're going to win with you, Jackie, because you are a terrific ballplayer.

JACKIE: I'll do my best, sir.

RICKEY: Your girl, what's her name?

JACKIE: Rae…Rachael.

RICKEY: Yes, Rae. You go and call her and ask her to marry you. You're going to need a good woman beside you. This is not going to be easy.

JACKIE: Thank you, Mr. Rickey. Thank you for having faith in me.

(JACKIE exits, elated. RUTH crosses back into the office and the interview continues.)

RICKEY: Jackie was sent to Jacksonville, Florida, to join the team for spring training. The team's manager was Clay Hopper.

(Enter HOPPER as RICKEY joins him and they survey the players.)

RICKEY: There's your new player. What do you think?

HOPPER: Please don't do this to me, Mr. Rickey. I'm from Mississippi. I was born and raised there. If you hire a colored boy to play on my team, my family and I will be run out of the state.

RICKEY: That's ridiculous, Mr. Hopper. Look at that man play. Look at that. He is absolutely superhuman!

HOPPER: Mr. Rickey, you really believe that niggers are human beings?

RICKEY: Yes I do, Mr. Hopper. And it is your responsibility to make sure that Robinson and twenty-four other human beings have a successful season.

HOPPER: Mr. Rickey, you hired me to manage your team and to win games. That's just what I intend to do. But nothin' says I have to like any of these ballplayers. OK boys, let's head out. We got a game tomorrow in Atlanta.

RADIO: *(Voice-over.)* This is WSS Atlanta with a sports bulletin. The exhibition game between the Montreal Royals and the Atlanta Browns has been canceled.

(During the radio announcement JACKIE, HOPPER, and AL walk to sign reading: "Game canceled, stadium lights out.")

JACKIE: What's going on? Are we in the right place?

AL: Where are all the fans?

HOPPER: Place looks shut up tight. Hey, wait a minute. *(Reads.)* "Game canceled. Stadium lights out."

AL: That's ridiculous.

JACKIE: What difference does that make? It's a day game!

(A pause as HOPPER looks at JACKIE.)

HOPPER: Come on boys. Let's go.

ANNOUNCER: *(Voice-over.)* This is WKKC, Fairmont, Virginia. Today at our very own county fairgrounds, the Montreal Royals will play an inter-squad game at 1:00 PM. It's free, so come one, come all—

(Players assemble on playing field during announcement.)

HOPPER: Robinson, you're up. *(To AL.)* Al, I want you to give Jackie a taste of what it's gonna be like out there during the regular season. I want you to brush him back.

AL: Brush him back? I can't do that, sir!

HOPPER: You can, and you will if you want to play for me. You got that?

AL: Yes, sir.

HOPPER: Robinson, let's see what ya got.

ANNOUNCER: *(Voice-over.)* Now batting for the Montreal Royals, Jackie Robinson.

(The sound of an angry, ugly crowd jeering JACKIE. AL pitches and misses the plate completely.)

HOPPER: Where're you throwing that ball, Campanis?

JACKIE: You wanna warm up?

AL: No, I'm all right.

HOPPER: *(To AL.)* Do what I told you.

(AL's second pitch hits JACKIE in the head.)

HOPPER: Good Lord, you all right, Robinson? *(To AL.)* What's wrong with you, Campanis? I told you to brush him back!

JACKIE: What?

HOPPER: You'll be all right. Rub some grass on it.

AL: You all right, Robinson?

JACKIE: Yeah.

HOPPER: Now put it across the plate.

(JACKIE hits the third pitch out of the park and the crowd becomes silent.)

ANNOUNCER: *(Voice-over.)* Well, I'll be. That nigger just hit a home run!

(Players cross into a restaurant. Sound of country music. The WAITRESS crosses on slowly.)

AL: I sure could use something to eat.

HOPPER: You can sit with us, Robinson.

WAITRESS: Evenin' fellas. Ya'll ready to order? Special today is liver 'n onions.

HOPPER: I'll have the tuna casserole and a hot, black coffee.

JACKIE: I'll have the liver and onions, and a vanilla milkshake and some fries.

WAITRESS: We don't serve your kind here. You see that sign?

(She points to a sign: "No coloreds served.")

JACKIE: What kinda sense does that make?

WAITRESS: Listen mister, I don't want no trouble. I'll call the sheriff if I have to—

HOPPER: Now, hang on, hang on, little lady. We don't want no trouble. Robinson—if you wouldn't mind.

JACKIE: I'll wait on the bus. I wasn't that hungry anyway.

(He exits.)

HOPPER: That's a good boy.

WAITRESS: May I take your order, sir?

AL: I'll have a double burger and liver 'n onions. And a vanilla milkshake and another vanilla milkshake. And fries, *two* orders of fries. I'm real hungry.

WAITRESS: Hungry enough for two.

(WAITRESS exits and then returns with food during JACKIE's speech. JACKIE is composing a letter.)

JACKIE: Dear Momma. Just a few lines to let you know how everything's going. Well, it's going. I never dreamed the road would be this rough. Rae's fine. She worries about me too much. Lord knows I do enough worrying for the both of us. I haven't been eating like I should and I've been finding it real hard to sleep at night. Momma, I've seen so much anger and hatred in its worst form since I've been on the road. But I take it. I've discovered a restraint in myself that I never knew I had—

AL: *(Crossing onto the bus with food for JACKIE.)* Still hungry?

JACKIE: You didn't have to do that. I appreciate it though.

AL: No problem. Listen, I'm sorry about what happened at yesterday's game. Is your ear OK?

JACKIE: What? I can't hear outta this ear. I got hit by a ball.

(AL finally realizes JACKIE is joking, and they both laugh.)

AL: Don't do that to me!

JACKIE: I'm fine. Just one of those accidents.

AL: It wasn't an accident. Hopper told me to brush you back.

JACKIE: Why?

AL: To give you a taste of what you'll be getting throughout the season. I can't control the ball under that kind of pressure. I'm sorry.

JACKIE: Thanks for telling me. You know, I just don't understand what makes one man think that he is so much better than another just because of the color of his skin. Why can't we all be neutral like a gray or something.

(JACKIE sees the humor in what he has said. They share a laugh.)

AL: *(Standing to go.)* Jackie, I want you to know that I wouldn't have the guts to do what you're doing.

JACKIE: Thank you, Al. *(AL exits.)* Dear Momma. This is going to be a long battle, but I know that with you and Rae and Mr. Rickey and the Lord giving me strength and inspiration, I can win.

(AL and HOPPER shift benches into beds. They are sleeping.)

JACKIE: We've just stopped in Syracuse at the Summit Hotel. They don't let Negroes stay there. That just tears me apart. Sometimes I think of how you told me that the Lord made black folks as a challenge and if we meet this challenge, it would make better people of us. Momma, pray I meet this challenge. Tomorrow, we play our first game in Montreal. I'm real nervous. I'll call you soon. I love you. Your son, Jackie.

(Transition to Montreal ballpark as RICKEY crosses to JACKIE.)

RICKEY: Welcome to Montreal, Jackie. It's good to see you.

JACKIE: I'm glad you could make it, Mr. Rickey.

RICKEY: I wouldn't have missed it for the world. How are you?

JACKIE: I'm nervous.

RICKEY: I'm not surprised. You just go out there and make me proud of you.

JACKIE: I will, Mr. Rickey.

(RICKEY becomes the pitcher as he describes JACKIE's first Montreal game. We hear the crowd cheering.)

RICKEY: Jackie's first game seemed like something out of a storybook. Pure magic! No one knew what would happen when Robinson stepped onto that field. Imagine how he felt when he was met by thousands and thousands of people cheering him, applauding and shouting, "Jackie, Jackie!!" Those shouts were music to our ears, an answer to our prayers. Now, that pitcher did not know what to think of Jackie and the cheering Montreal crowd. When he pitched Jackie that first ball, *(Crack.)*. Jackie lined it into right field for a double.

(JACKIE runs to second base in slow motion.)

RICKEY: That pitcher knew Jackie's reputation for base stealing and he knew he was in the hot seat. And there was Jackie, circling his base like a tiger ready to pounce. When that pitcher finally let one fly, Jackie raced for third.

(JACKIE races for third.)

RICKEY: He was safe! The pitcher was dizzy with nervousness. But *nobody* steals home. Then, as he wound up his arm, Jackie danced into home!

(JACKIE steals home. AL and HOPPER lift him onto their shoulders.)

RICKEY: After the game, the crowd went crazy. They were on their feet screaming, laughing, crying. They swooped onto the field, lifted Jackie onto their shoulders and carried him off crying, "Jackie, Jackie, Jackie!!"

(Players carry JACKIE off. JACKIE and AL slip into a restaurant to avoid the crowd of enthusiastic fans.)

AL: He went that-a-way! *(Jokingly imitating the fans.)* Jackie! Jackie! *(To crowd.)* Bye.

JACKIE: *(Pulling AL into restaurant.)* Get in here!

AL: I think you're safe from your fans here.

JACKIE: I never thought I'd be running from a crowd that loves me. Usually, they want to lynch me. *(They laugh.)*

AL: Let's get something to eat.

JACKIE: Yeah, this looks great. I'm gonna try the chicken.

(They are serving themselves cafeteria style. The CASHIER enters and tries to maintain her composure.)

AL: Think I'll stick to the hamburgers.

JACKIE: These potatoes look good, and beans—

CASHIER: *(A French Canadian.)* I am sorry, sir. We cannot serve you here.

JACKIE: Not again.

CASHIER: Your money is no good here.

JACKIE: What's wrong with my money?

CASHIER: *(Melting.)* Because you are Jackie Robinson. And here, Jackie Robinson will always eat free!

JACKIE: Thanks.

CASHIER: May I have your autograph, *Monsieur?*

JACKIE: Sure.

CASHIER: "To Michellette." *Merci, Monsieur.* And may I have a kiss? *(She offers JACKIE her hand.)*

JACKIE: Of course, *Mademoiselle.*

(JACKIE gallantly kisses her hand.)

CASHIER: *(Overwhelmed.)* Oh, *Monsieur* Robinson.

AL: *(Passing her.)* I'm on the team, too.

CASHIER: *Un petit moment, Monsieur.* That will be eighty-five cents.

AL: I'm a Montreal Royal, too.

CASHIER: Eighty-five cents, *s'il vous plaît.*

JACKIE: Pay the lady.

(AL pays her, to JACKIE's playful delight. RICKEY crosses in and the scene changes. CASHIER exits as AL, HOPPER, and JACKIE cross in slow motion raising their hands triumphantly in a sign of "We're number 1!")

RICKEY: That season with Montreal surpassed even my greatest hopes for Jackie. His statistics were unbelievable: .349 batting average, 113 RBIs, a .984 fielding *and* the Montreal Royals won the Little World Series.

(A cheer from players. RICKEY exits as HOPPER gathers players.)

HOPPER: Everybody sit down, sit down! I want to say a few words to y'all. When we started out this season, things weren't easy. Having Jackie on our team meant we had to put up with more stunts and trouble and downright hate than any other ball club before us. But let me be the first to say, that having Jackie on our team has also given us the privilege of playing with one of the best ballplayers I've ever seen. Now, I know I've learned something this season—about what it takes to win. You're a winner, Jackie, and a fine gentleman.

(He offers his hand to JACKIE.)

JACKIE: *(Shaking HOPPER's hand.)* Thank you, sir.

HOPPER: Let's go out and meet the press.

(AL runs off but HOPPER stops JACKIE.)

HOPPER: Jackie, Mr. Rickey wanted me to tell you that you're gonna be playing for Brooklyn next year, son. And I want you to know, well, if things don't work out in Brooklyn you can always play for me, anytime.

JACKIE: Thank you, sir.

HOPPER: Good luck, son.

(HOPPER exits and RICKEY enters.)

RICKEY: Welcome to Brooklyn, Jackie. You glad to be here?

JACKIE: To tell you the truth, sir, no. I like Montreal. The fans like me. Rae's happy there and I hear the Dodgers don't want me playin' with them.

RICKEY: Come on, Jackie. *(They exit.)*

PEE WEE: *(Entering.)* Come on, Dixie. I can't believe you're gonna do a thing like this.

DIXIE: *(Voice-over.)* I ain't playin' with no nigger. I'll be the first to sign that petition.

ANOTHER: *(Voice-over.)* I'll be the second. We're gonna get Mr. Rickey to get that boy outta here. You with us, Pee Wee?

PEE WEE: Look, boys. I wanna play baseball. The Dodgers are my job. I'll play with anyone who'll keep my family fed. I ain't signing no petition! *(DUROCHER enters and overhears what is going on.)*

DIXIE: *(Voice-over.)* Well, so long, Pee Wee. Cause if that boy *does* come here, I'm gonna ask to be traded.

DUROCHER: Well! Some of you boys don't want to play with Robinson. A petition, huh.

DIXIE: *(Voice-over.)* What's it to you, Mr. Durocher?

DUROCHER: Cause I'm the manager of this ball club and I'm only interested in one thing—*winning*. I'll play an elephant if he can do the job. And to make room for him, I'll send my own brother home. Dixie, if you want be traded, just mention it to Mr. Rickey and you're *gone*. So make up your minds to it, boys. Robinson is a good ballplayer. He's gonna put money in your pockets and money in mine. And for all I hear, he's only the first. There's plenty more coming right behind him. They have the talent and they are coming to play. Unless you fellas wake up, they're gonna run you right outta the ballpark. Now, I don't want to see another petition. This meeting is over. *(He exits with PEE WEE.)*

RICKEY: *(Entering with RUTH.)* No one was prepared for what 1947 brought to the Dodgers. Jackie had to face unbelievable abuse. He cracked under the pressure.

(JACKIE enters the office.)

JACKIE: Mr. Rickey. I've been looking all over for you. I've got to talk to you.

RICKEY: What's the matter, Jackie? You're shaking all over.

Most Valuable Player 21

JACKIE: It's Rae. When I got home last night she was crying like crazy. I tried to calm her down, but she just kept shaking and crying.

RICKEY: What happened?

JACKIE: She was walking home with the baby, and somebody hollered out of a car, "Your Daddy's a dead man, nigger boy."

RICKEY: Good Lord.

JACKIE: It wasn't the first time, Mr. Rickey, but it shook her up real bad. She's scared for our baby. I'm scared. My family is in danger because of me.

RICKEY: I didn't want this to happen.

JACKIE: I need some time away from baseball.

RICKEY: Don't give in now, Jackie.

JACKIE: I can't have my son growing up afraid!

RICKEY: He will grow up with the knowledge that his father has tremendous courage.

JACKIE: I swear, Mr. Rickey. Sometimes I feel like this is more your cause than mine. Why? Why is this so important to you?!

RICKEY: When I was a student at Ohio Wesleyan, I was also the coach of the baseball team. One night we were on the road, getting ready to play Notre Dame. When we got to our hotel, the room clerk refused to allow the team's catcher to register. Our catcher was a Negro, and one of the finest young men I've ever known. That didn't matter to that room clerk. His hotel was for "whites only." I finally convinced him to let the young man sleep in my room, but by the time I'd finished registering the team and got up to my room, I found that young man in there crying. Crying as if his heart would break. He was desperately pulling at his skin, scratching away at his own skin, saying, "If I could just tear it off, I'd be like everyone else. It's just my skin. It's my *skin*, Mr. Rickey." That night, I promised myself that I would fight prejudice for the rest of my life. I can't do it alone, either, Jackie.

JACKIE: I know.

RICKEY: There is no way I can know how much you are hurting. God made me white, and right now that makes it easier. But I do know the pain of having to live in a world that doesn't match my dreams.

JACKIE: What would you do if it were your son?

RICKEY: I'd like to think I'd go out onto that ball field and block out all the ugliness and hate, and send that ball out of the park with all my strength. You do what you have to Jackie. It's up to you.

(RICKEY exits. JACKIE is alone. He begins to hear angry voices in his mind.)

VOICE: *(Voice-over.)* Hey, nigger. Why don't you go back to the cotton fields where you belong!

ANOTHER: *(Voice-over.)* They're waiting for you in the jungles, black boy.

RAE: *(Voice-over.)* It's all right, Jackie. I'm with you, honey.

VOICE: *(Voice-over.)* We don't want you here, nigger.

RAE: *(Voice-over.)* You're not alone, baby. I believe in you.

VOICE: *(Voice-over.)* Back to the bushes, nigger boy.

RAE: *(Voice-over.)* I love you, Jackie. We can do this together.

(By the end of the sequence, JACKIE is standing with his bat, triumphantly.)

JACKIE: Send it out of the park.

(CRACK! JACKIE swings with all his might. RICKEY enters with RUTH as interview continues. The players are assembling on the field.)

RICKEY: Our first series in St. Louis was the lowest point in Jackie's first season. Before the second game, the St. Louis players tried to boycott. I called Ford Frick, President of the National League, who issued the following statement: "If you don't play, you will be suspended for life."

(In all the following baseball sequences, the players create the plays that the radio describes. The slow motion begins with the crack of the bat, and real motion resumes once a play is completed.)

RADIO: *(Voice-over.)* Leading off first for Brooklyn, Jackie Robinson. Enos Blackwell rocks and delivers. Whoa—it's up and right in on Robinson, brushing him back. Robinson is back in the box.

JACKIE: *(Who has taken an angry step toward ENOS BLACKWELL, now steps back to the box.)* Send it out of the park…send it out of the park.

RADIO: *(Voice-over.)* Blackwell fires. *(CRACK.)* It's a long fly ball, deep into center field. Still going, going, it's a home run. Robinson hits his first home run of the series.

(Dodgers go to outfield and St. Louis is at bat.)

RADIO: *(Voice-over.)* Going into the bottom of the fifth, Blackwell up to bat for St. Louis. There's the pitch. *(CRACK.)* It's a shot up the middle. Blackwell is on his way to second.

ENOS: *(Pushing JACKIE.)* Outta my way, nigger.

PEE WEE: Why don't you pick on somebody who can yell back at ya, Enos. Try callin' me names and see what happens.

ENOS: Never thought you'd be such a nigger lover, Pee Wee.

PEE WEE: Get off it, Enos. He'll pound your red neck into the ground no matter what color he is.

ENOS: Ain't no nigger showin' me up.

RADIO: *(Voice-over.)* The count's 0 and 1. Here's the pitch. *(CRACK.)* A solid drive down the line. It's gloved by Robinson. He fires to Reese covering second, catching Blackwell off the bag. It's another Robinson-Reese double play!

PEE WEE: *(Gloating.)* You're out, Enos.

RADIO: *(Voice-over.)* Bottom of the ninth. Dodgers ahead 4 to 3 but the Cards are threatening with one out and men on first and third. Blackwell to the plate. Here's the pitch. *(CRACK.)* There's a shot right at Robinson. He grabs it, steps on first, double play, and the Dodgers win 4 to 3. Hey, Blackwell has spiked Robinson. There's a fight on the field. The Dodgers are pouring out of their dugout.

ENOS: What do you think of that, nigger?

PEE WEE: Get off the field you ignorant S.O.B!

RICKEY: *(Overlapping.)* I'll see you never play professional baseball again, Blackwell.

PEE WEE: *(Overlapping.)* Get outta here, ya bum!

ENOS: I want that nigger to know what the St. Louis Cardinals think of him. He ain't never playin' this game. It's a white man's game, nigger!

RICKEY: Before the third game, Enos and his teammates brought Jackie a gift.

ENOS: *(Crossing to the Dodgers' dugout.)* Hey, Pee Wee. Sorry 'bout yesterday. The spikin' and all. No hard feelings. We wanted Jackie to have this so he'll know just what the Cardinals think of him.

PEE WEE: What is it, Enos?

ENOS: Oh, Jackie'll recognize him—uh, *it.* See ya.

PEE WEE: I don't know, Mr. Rickey. I think we should open it.

RICKEY: *(As PEE WEE opens it.)* Judas priest!

PEE WEE: Good God Almighty! It's a dead cat!

ENOS: That's one dead black cat to another. If he ain't careful, he'll wind up that way, too.

PEE WEE: That's pretty sick, Enos.

RICKEY: Before the fourth game the St. Louis police received a death threat, saying that Jackie would be shot from the crowd during the third inning.

RADIO: *(Voice-over.)* There's an air of anxiety here today. The entire stadium is wondering if Robinson will come up to bat.

RICKEY: I can't let you play, Jackie.

JACKIE: Mr. Rickey, they can't get rid of me this easy. I'll play till I hear the gun.

RICKEY: Don't be a fool!

JACKIE: Come on, Mr. Rickey. This is what you warned me about. They're trying to threaten me outta playing baseball.

RICKEY: There are a lot of crazy people out here. It's not worth the chance!

JACKIE: I gotta do it. Besides, they ain't supposed to shoot me till the third inning.

RADIO: *(Voice-over.)* Robinson is due up for the Dodgers. Yes, he is heading for the plate.

ENOS: Stay low, Robinson.

RADIO: *(Voice-over.)* Blackwell winds and delivers. *(CRACK.)* Robinson pops it up in front of the mound. Blackwell's there—

ENOS: I got it!

RADIO: *(Voice-over.)* Makes the catch!

ENOS: Great hit, dead meat.

RADIO *(Voice-over.)* Moving into the bottom of the second inning. The pressure on these boys must be tremendous. There seems to be a delay with the Dodgers taking the field. We don't see Robinson. Here comes Pee Wee Reese escorting Jackie to first base.

PEE WEE: *(Comically covering JACKIE as they walk.)* If they're gonna shoot you, Buddy, they're gonna have to kill us both.

JACKIE: Go on, Pee Wee, go play shortstop.

RADIO: *(Voice-over.)* Scheduled to lead off at the top of the third inning is Jackie Robinson. But it's anybody's guess if he'll play the inning.

RICKEY: Jackie, this is crazy. I'm taking you out of the game.

JACKIE: Mr. Rickey, if I give in this time, there's gonna be a letter in every town we play in, hoping to make me back down. I'm not gonna live with that.

RICKEY: The risk is too great!

JACKIE: And I've been fighting too long to back down now. Nobody's keeping me from doing my job.

RICKEY: Jackie, please!

JACKIE: Let me do this!

PEE WEE: Come on, Buddy, don't be stupid—

RADIO: *(Voice-over.)* Ladies and gentlemen, here comes Jackie Robinson to the plate. The crowd is on their feet. The courage of this man is incredible.

ENOS: *Bang*, Robinson.

JACKIE: If they're gonna shoot me, they're gonna have to hit a movin' target. *(To himself.)* Send it out of the park. Send it out of the park.

RADIO: *(Voice-over.)* Blackwell from the stretch. He delivers. *(CRACK.)* It's a blast up the middle for a base hit. But Robinson is not slowing down. He's headed for second. The throw is coming in but Robinson is running flat out toward third. The second baseman bobbles the ball. Robinson rounds third, heading toward the plate. There's the throw. Robinson slides ahead of the throw. Robinson comes all the way in to score!

JACKIE: This is it, Mr. Rickey. Nothin's gonna stop us now. We're going straight to the top.

(JACKIE and PEE WEE celebrate, then exit under RICKEY's speech to set up the awards ceremony.)

RICKEY: The 1947 Dodgers were a truly integrated team if there ever was one. An Italian in left field, a Pole at second base, a southerner as shortstop and now Jackie Robinson at first base—a leader and an inspiration to his teammates. His batting average for '47 was .297 and he led the leagues with twenty-nine stolen bases. Unfortunately, this was not enough to overcome the jinx of the New York Yankees in the World Series. They beat us four games to three. But at the end of the season, I had the pleasure of presenting Jackie with the coveted title of Rookie of the Year.

(JACKIE and PEE WEE are seated together. ENOS sits separately. RICKEY crosses to the podium.)

RICKEY: It gives me great personal joy to be here tonight to honor a young man who has changed the face of baseball. A young man who has returned harshness with hitting, racial hatred with RBIs. A young man I have come to hold as dear to me as a son. With deepest pride and pleasure, I present the 1947 Rookie of the Year Award to Mr. Jackie Robinson.

(JACKIE and RICKEY shake hands. JACKIE crosses to podium.)

JACKIE: Thank you. I'm not a great speech maker, but this one will be easy because what I have to say is very important to me. First I would like to thank my teammates, like Pee Wee Reese, who stood beside me down a long road. It's been a privilege to play with such fine ballplayers

(As he shakes PEE WEE's hand, JACKIE hears voices from his memory. PEE WEE exits.)

DIXIE: *(Voice-over.)* I ain't playing with no nigger.

PEE WEE: *(Voice-over.)* I ain't signin' no petition.

JACKIE: And to Mr. Rickey, thank you for believing in me. You've been the father I never had. You've helped me to see that my game was the best way to fight back against hate and prejudice.

(JACKIE shakes hands, then embraces RICKEY. RICKEY exits.)

VOICE: *(Voice-over.)* Hey, nigger. What kinda coward are you?

ANOTHER: *(Voice-over.)* You like catchin' bottles in the face?

JACKIE: And thank you too, Enos Blackwell, for testing every ounce of control I got.

(He offers ENOS his hand, but ENOS refuses to shake his hand and walks out.)

JACKIE: And someday, you're gonna see my strength in all its glory, riding down on you so hard, it'll make your head spin!

RAE: *(Voice-over.)* Jackie, honey. Your temper is your worst enemy. If you don't learn to control it—

MOMMA: *(Voice-over.)* Son, don't let that bull head of yours go flyin' off the handle.

JACKIE: And thank you, too, Momma for putting me on the right track. And my wife, Rae, for keeping me on that train. I couldn't have done it without you. And finally, to all you people who came out to cheer me on— *(JACKIE hears voices of jeers and abuse.)* And to all you people who heckled me, called me every dirty name you could dredge up: Thank you, too, for making me rage inside. For making me ready to break out of the batting cage and knock some sense into every one of you. To get you to look with your hearts and not just with your blind eyes. I didn't do this to be a martyr or a hero, but to give my son the chance—should he decide to play baseball or any other sport—the chance to be judged not by the color of his skin, but by his ability to play and the strength of his character. At least I've saved him the humiliation of being the first Negro to break into a white man's game. But that's changed now. The game belongs to everybody—Negro players and Negro fans, too. But we still got a long way to go. For my people, thank you. For my people…

(JACKIE begins to run around the field—just as we saw him at the beginning of the play. RICKEY and RUTH cross into RICKEY's office.)

RICKEY: That was his '47 season. This year, Jackie's problems began with his coming in overweight at the top of training camp. Too many meals on the banquet circuit! He fought it and won, but all season he played almost too hard, like he was trying to make up for lost time.

RUTH: How terribly sad. Well, Mr. Rickey, I shan't take anymore of your time. It's been lovely to meet you. I'm sure my story will absolutely delight the readers of the *Times*.

RICKEY: It's been my pleasure, Miss Warton.

RUTH: Thank you, again. And please give my best to Mr. Robinson. His courage is extraordinary—a kind that all can admire, whether one follows baseball or not. He must be a remarkable gentleman.

RICKEY: He is, Miss Warton.

(RUTH exits. RICKEY turns and sees JACKIE in his office.)

RICKEY: Jackie! Judas Priest! You look like you've been through the wringer. Sit down.

JACKIE: I'm no good for the team, Mr. Rickey. I can't pull my weight. I'm gonna be quittin'.

RICKEY: What are you talking about?

JACKIE: I can't keep up! My game is slipping. I'm gonna make room for better ballplayers and retire.

RICKEY: You're twenty-nine years old and you want to retire? Jackie, you just had a season that would have thrilled most other ballplayers.

JACKIE: That's not good enough for me. Besides, you don't need me anymore. You got Roy Campanella. Let him be your token Negro. I can't take it anymore. To stand up to a punch in the gut with silence?! It's breakin' me, Mr. Rickey. I ain't gonna be your strong silent Negro player no more.

RICKEY: You think I used you to crack the ice and now I'm going to throw you away? You are a valuable member of this team, Mr. Robinson. No token Negro. I have asked you to stand up to the most difficult challenges I have ever asked a player to face. To endure the humiliations you have had to suffer—it's broken my heart to stand by and watch it happen. But it *had* to happen, Jackie, to help the world see past the color of your skin. Through your strength, you have opened the gates. Now the Dodgers are just one of several teams in the major league with Negro players. You've *done* it, Jackie! *(Pause.)* So the next time anyone throws a punch in your gut, OK. It's your choice. You've got your freedom. You've earned it. Fight back like any other player. You're your own man now. Get into as much trouble as you like.

JACKIE: That'll make the difference, Mr. Rickey.

RICKEY: Thought it might. Good night, Jackie.

(RICKEY exits.)

JACKIE: All right. All right!! No more "noble experiment!" Lord, it's gonna feel good to let 'em know I am not gonna take it anymore. It's been all bottled up inside me. That's been my trouble. Now I can bust out! Be just another ballplayer, fightin' back when it's unfair. When Bobby Bragen pushes somebody for knockin' him down, does he get thrown out of the game? That's what I'll do. Pee Wee yells back when somebody hollers something at him. I'll yell back, too! That's what I'll do. You hear that, Campy? And old Sachel Page over at the Indians, and all you other Negro players? We are not the long suffering examples anymore, brothers. We are just ballplayers! Ballplayers! And Jackie Robinson's gonna be the best ballplayer in the major leagues. I ain't givin' up, Momma! I'm goin' straight to the top in '49!

(The stage is transformed to ball field. Players assemble. RUTH watches the baseball games from the stands.)

RADIO: *(Voice-over.)* April 3, 1949. Ladies and gentlemen, welcome to opening day here at Ebbets Field, where the Brooklyn Dodgers play host to the St. Louis Cardinals. Leading off for Brooklyn, second baseman, Jackie Robinson.

ENOS: *(From the mound.)* Welcome back, chocolate drop.

PEE WEE: Aw, stick to the game, Enos.

JACKIE: Just give me something I can hit, you hick.

ENOS: I ain't givin' you nothin'.

RADIO: *(Voice-over.)* Blackwell looks in. He's set. Here's the pitch—called—strike one!

ENOS: What do you want, chocolate drop, the ball on a silver platter?

JACKIE: I'm serving this up to you, white boy, straight up the middle.

RADIO: *(Voice-over.)* Blackwell back on the rubber. Here's the 0-1 delivery. *(CRACK.)* There's a smash up the middle. In for a base—no, Robinson's rounding first—he's going for two. And Robinson is in with a double.

JACKIE: What's the matter there, Enos? You a little slow? Did you gain a little weight? Ha. Ha!

ENOS: Not as much as you, fat mouth.

RADIO: *(Voice-over.)* Now batting for Brooklyn, short stop, Number 1, Pee Wee Reese. Blackwell sets, rocks and delivers. Swing and a miss. Strike one!

JACKIE: Take your time, buddy, take your time.

ENOS: Shut your mouth, boy.

JACKIE: *(Shouting.)* All right, buddy, let's pick a good one!

RADIO: Reese digging in—Blackwell with the 0-1 delivery. Whoa!! It's up and in. Pee Wee dives out of the way.

PEE WEE *(Recovering.)* What's your beef, Enos?

ENOS: Hey, I didn't mean it, nigger-lover.

(PEE WEE charges toward ENOS, but JACKIE gets there first.)

JACKIE: Don't you ever try anything like that on any of my teammates again, cause if you do, you can forget about crossing Brooklyn's second base, cause I'll be there to ram my glove down your throat. Got it?

RADIO: *(Voice-over.)* May 28, 1949. The National League race is a tight one with the Dodgers and Cards tied for first. Time out has been called here in the ninth with the Dodgers and Cards tied at three each. Blackwell is talking over strategy with Eddy Dyer, manager of the Cardinals. Blackwell is heading back to the mound, and play will resume. Pee Wee Reese up to bat. Here's Blackwell with the offering. Low and away. Ball one!

JACKIE: Way to watch it, Pee Wee. Way to watch it. Hit me home, Harold.

RICKEY: Come on, Pee Wee. You know what to do.

RADIO: *(Voice-over.)* Blackwell looks in. Robinson with a good lead off third. There's the wind up—Robinson is breaking for home. The catcher tries to tag him out, but Robinson is safe! The Dodgers are ahead by one, but the Cards have the meat of the order coming up in the ninth. Hey, Pee Wee is down. Looks like a bottle from the stands.

JACKIE: *(To the crowd.)* Why don't you keep your garbage to yourself! You think it's funny catching bottles in the head? This is a playing field not trash heap. I'll break the next person's arm who throws anything on this field.

ENOS: *(Overlapping JACKIE's lines.)* If anybody throws another piece of trash on this field, you're gonna answer to me. We ain't puttin' up with this. We can bust heads for this—

(ENOS and JACKIE notice that each is yelling at the crowd—an awkward acknowledgment that they are actually on the same side of an argument.)

JACKIE: We'll have you thrown out on your ear.

ENOS: He's darn right we will.

RADIO: *(Voice-over.)* July 5, 1949. This all-star game is a fight to the end. The National League is holding on to a one run lead. But on the field today, we see longtime rivals turn teammates for a day—Jackie Robinson and Enos Blackwell. Stan Musial is holding Larry Dobson of the Indians tight on the bag at first. DiMaggio steps up to the plate.

Blackwell rocks and delivers. *(CRACK.)* It's a shot between first and second. Robinson and Musial both dive for the ball. Robinson's up with it, rolls, fires to Pee Wee at second for one, back to Blackwell covering first. Double play! And the National League winds this 1949 all-star game.

PEE WEE: All right!

ENOS: I don't see plays like that too often, Robinson. You're all right.

JACKIE: Way to cover first, Enos. Let's do it again sometime.

(ENOS extends his hand to help JACKIE to his feet. JACKIE takes it.)

RUTH: This is Ruth Warton in America reporting live for the BBC. *(During RUTH's speech, the stage is set for the awards ceremony.)* Dateline: October 15, 1949. The air is filled with anticipation tonight here at the annual banquet of the Sports Writers of America, where the prestigious award of this year's "Most Valuable Player" will be presented. I cannot deny my personal hope that the title will go to a superb athlete whom I have had the pleasure of following throughout the past year—play by play, prejudice by prejudice, triumph by triumph. And now, stepping up to the podium to present the award, Mr. Branch Rickey.

(RICKEY steps up to the podium.)

RICKEY: Every baseball player dreams of this moment. Of hearing his name called in front of this prestigious gathering of his colleagues. Of knowing that all the hours, the sweat, and even the tears have been worth it. Ladies and gentlemen, I have the honor of presenting this year's "Most Valuable Player" award to Jackie Robinson.

(Great cheers. JACKIE steps up to the podium.)

JACKIE: Thank you, Mr. Rickey. My Momma used to say, "Don't nothin' good come outta this world unless you have to suffer a little." *(Jokes.)* Well, this award is something *really* good for *lots* of suffering. But I'm awfully proud. And you're right, Mr. Rickey. It has been worth it. And I thank you, and lots of other people, for giving me the breaks and opportunities that no Negro player has ever had before me. *(Pause.)* Guess the newspapers tomorrow will say I've made it. But, I have always known in my heart that my success won't mean anything till the humblest Negro kid has made it, too. When my children can go to school next to white children, can ride with dignity on the front seat of a bus; can play with children of all races on a playground, even sit in the same row in the movie house rather than bein' stuck up in the balcony, even be free to use the same public rest rooms without a sign hangin' over the door saying "whites only." These are my dreams, but my dreams don't stop there. They won't stop until every person living on this earth is free to choose the life he wants to lead, the friends he wants to have, and the God he wants to worship, regardless of the color of his skin.

(All players take places on the field, and JACKIE delivers his final speech as he rounds the bases for home. All players are in slow motion.)

JACKIE: I don't know. Maybe I'm asking for changes that only a politician can make. And Lord knows I'm no politician. But I have changed things— with my glove and with my bat. I don't know what my playin's gonna mean to anybody in the future, *(CRACK.)* but I know what it means to me. *(JACKIE is now on first base.)*

It means I'm not gonna give up until every barrier that separates race from race comes tumblin' down. My spirit's gonna be there. Every time a black child, a Mexican child, *any* child gets—*(JACKIE runs to second base.)* a door slammed in his face, I'll be standing right beside him. Until every injustice that— *(JACKIE runs to third base.)* —robs a human being of his dignity is wiped off the face of this earth, Jackie Robinson's gonna be there, battin' a thousand for anybody who needs me. Cause I'm a Robinson— *(He slides into home.)*

CAST: Safe!!

JACKIE: And Robinsons don't give up!!

(The cast assembles in a circle, piling their hands on top of one another, then shout "Break.")

END OF PLAY

Prodigy

TO
FINN, MICHAEL,
SEAN, AND KEVIN,
ALWAYS

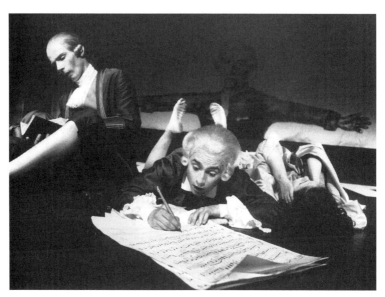

Dominik Castell as Leopold Mozart, Gokhan Bolcan as Wolfgang Mozart, and Kathrin Irion as Nannerl Mozart in Prodigy *at Theater der Stadt, Heidelberg, Germany, 1991. Photo by Gudrun Holde Ortner.*

ORIGINAL PRODUCTION

Prodigy was commissioned by the California Theatre Center and first performed, under the title of *Young Mozart,* at the California Theatre Center on April 8, 1986, under the direction of Sean Michael Dowse. The cast was as follows:

LEOPOLD MOZART . . . . Kevin Reese
WOLFGANG MOZART. . . . . Kevin Davis
ANNA MARIA MOZART . . . . Tracy Huffman
NANNERL MOZART . . . . Becky Steuben
COURTIERS. David Gassner, Brian Lewis
                                        Pat Sibley, Dorien Wilson

Set Design. . . . . Michael R. Cook
Costume Design . . . . Colleen Troy
                                                Michael R. Cook
Sound Design . . . . Jeffra Cook
Light Design. . . . . Jon Kranbuhl
Stage Manager . . . . Maureen Chapman
General Director, California Theatre Center. . . . Gayle Cornelison

Prodigy was presented by the John F. Kennedy Center for the Performing Arts Education Program through its Programs for Children and Youth, October 5–31, 1987, under the direction of Mary Hall Surface. The cast was as follows:

LEOPOLD MOZART . . . . Kevin Reese
WOLFGANG MOZART . . . . Joan L. Meyer
ANNA MARIA MOZART. . . . . Christi Engle
NANNERL MOZART . . . . Brande Martin
COURTIERS . . . . William Freimuth, Mykal Knight
                                Scott Morgan, Patricia Tuili-Hawkridge

Set Design. . . . . Michael Layton
Costume Design . . . . Catherine Adair
Lighting Design. . . . . Daniel MacLean Wagner
Sound Design . . . . Joseph Holt
Stage Manager . . . . James J. Taylor
Produced by . . . . Carole C. Sullivan

NOTES FOR *PRODIGY*

Prodigy was first performed by eight actors, the four Courtiers playing the numerous Kings, Queens, Gossips, and Messengers. The distinction of, for example, "Courtier One" in the script is not intended to designate one actor as Courtier One throughout the piece, but merely to distinguish one courtier from another in that particular sequence. (In the Kennedy Center production I chose to cast the same actor as each of the three kings, the same actress as the queens, and the same actor to play each of the Courtiers One and Two. This allowed each court scene to have a haunting sameness to Wolfgang; it also gave the actors a very interesting through-line with which to work, while creating distinctly different characters.)

Prodigy is often cast with the roles of Wolfgang and Nannerl Mozart played by children. For the young audience, the opportunity to identify with one of their own in such circumstances creates vivid exciting theater. I have also seen brilliantly conceived, highly theatrical productions of *Prodigy* in which all roles are played by adults.

The play should be considered as a piece of music—each scene following smoothly into the next, with minimal scenic adjustments. The original production dwelled in a set consisting of an ornate double-door upstage, two decorated columns down right and down left, and a painted floor—all marbled in Salzburg-pastel unity. A harpsichord on wheels was the central furniture piece with the occasional chair brought out for certain scenes. The visual emphasis should go to realizing the multileveled metaphor of the play, utilizing the puppets and the cutouts.

A musical score for the piece is available from Anchorage Press.

—*Mary Hall Surface*

CHARACTERS

WOLFGANG MOZART: A highly gifted child of six years (eight by the play's end)

LEOPOLD MOZART: Wolfgang's father, a court composer

NANNERL MOZART: A musically talented child of ten years (twelve by the play's end)

ANNA MARIA MOZART: Wife of Leopold, Mother of Wolfgang and Nannerl

ELECTORATE: A member of Munich's aristocracy

ELECTORATE'S WIFE: Charmed by the Mozart children

MUNICH COURTIER ONE: A know-it-all

MUNICH COURTIER TWO: Courtier One's competitor

FOUR GOSSIPS IN SALZBURG: Eager to fuel rumors while dancing their minuets

FRANCIS I: Emperor of Vienna

MARIA THERESA: Empress of Vienna

VIENNESE COURTIER ONE: Suspicious of Leopold's motives

VIENNESE COURTIER TWO: Similarly suspicious

MESSENGER: From the Court of Wurtemburg

LOUIS XV: King of France

QUEEN: Queen of France

COURTIER ONE: Servant to the king

COURTIER TWO: Servant to the king

FOUR GOSSIPS IN LONDON: Eager to fuel rumors while seated in their opera box

NOBILITY ONE: Member of London's aristocracy

NOBILITY TWO: Member of London's aristocracy

DAINES BARRINGTON: Distinguished historian and musician

PUBLISHER: A London Music publisher

Numerous Barkers, Innkeepers, Courtiers on the Grand Tour

SETTING

Salzburg, Austria. Then journeying from Munich, to Vienna, to Paris, to London, and points in between on the Mozart's first Grand Tour of Europe.

TIME

1762–1764

PRELUDE

Lights up, WOLFGANG, age 6, playfully runs on stage carrying his two puppets, as if hiding from his father. LEOPOLD enters and pursues WOLFGANG in a playful chase around the harpsichord. With much laughter, LEOPOLD catches his son. The puppets are then placed down lovingly. WOLFGANG and LEOPOLD embrace.

WOLFGANG: Good night, Poppa.

LEOPOLD: Good night, Son.

WOLFGANG: I love you.

LEOPOLD: And I love you, with all my heart.

(WOLFGANG snuggles into his father's arms to go to sleep. LEOPOLD begins to sing a simple melody, which will become the theme of the second movement of WOLFGANG's Symphony No. 4. Finishing the tune, LEOPOLD rocks WOLFGANG tenderly, and he begins to pray.)

LEOPOLD: Heavenly Father, how could I have been blessed with such a son? To guard such beauty, in a *child?* I pray for your guidance, dearest Lord, as I devote my life to my son—so that your great gift of his music can live for all time. Amen.

1. ALLEGRO

A burst of music. Actors, with handheld carnival masks, assemble on stage in an orchestrated fashion around a harpsichord. LEOPOLD MOZART, his wife, ANNA MARIA, and their children, WOLFGANG and NANNERL, age ten, assume their positions in a performance tableau. WOLFGANG is seated at the harpsichord, accompanied by his sister who is singing. WOLFGANG concludes the piece brilliantly to great applause. The children bow, then run to their parents' arms for a hug.

ELECTORATE: What extraordinary children, Herr Mozart.

ELECTORATE'S WIFE: And how sweet.

LEOPOLD: Thank you, sire. *(To WOLFGANG and NANNERL.)* That was beautiful, my dears.

ELECTORATE: It is truly remarkable that at such a tender age their musical accomplishments are so great.

LEOPOLD: My children surprise me daily, my lord.

(WOLFGANG crawls under the harpsichord to everyone's amusement.)

COURTIER ONE: Tell us, Herr Mozart. I have heard that the boy could distinguish the interval of a third on the harpsichord when he was only three years old.

LEOPOLD: I humbly admit that it is true.

COURTIER ONE: *(To COURTIER TWO.)* You see!

COURTIER TWO: But is it not mere rumor that at the age of four he could memorize a minuet and trio in an hour.

COURTIER ONE: A mere thirty minutes is what I have heard.

LEOPOLD: With awe, I tell you the latter is true. But now, my son has little need for the written music after *once* hearing the piece.

COURTIER TWO: It is a miracle!

LEOPOLD: A gift from God, surely, my lord.

(WOLFGANG curiously explores the room.)

ELECTORATE'S WIFE: How fascinating. *(To COURTIER ONE.)* Please, continue.

COURTIER ONE: The little girl, then. Do I understand that she has studied the keyboard instruments as well as having such a delightful little voice?

LEOPOLD: In truth, it was my instruction to Nannerl that first awakened the gift of music in my son. Wolfgang interrupted our lessons when he was only two insisting that he should be taught as well.

COURTIER TWO: Astonishing!

ELECTORATE: And taught him you have, Herr Mozart. Endless hours of instruction, I hear.

ANNA MARIA: My husband is the children's only teacher in all subjects.

LEOPOLD: God has made me the guardian of a great gift. I cannot allow his song from heaven not to be heard on earth.

ELECTORATE: But what of your position as court composer to the Archbishop of Salzburg, Herr Mozart? Surely the Archbishop does not allow his servants to neglect their duties for the sake of delighting us here in Munich?

LEOPOLD: By the Archbishop's generosity alone was this journey possible. I have been granted leave.

ANNA MARIA: With full pay.

ELECTORATE'S WIFE: So that you might share this miracle with our court during carnival? How charming.

COURTIER TWO: But I must ask, has this "child" actually composed a full concerto for the harpsichord?

LEOPOLD: With delight, I answer yes.

COURTIER ONE: I'm right again!

COURTIER TWO: But I cannot believe the story that the child can name any pitch which is played, while not looking at the keyboard.

WOLFGANG: I can.

LEOPOLD: *(To WOLFGANG.) Sire!*

WOLFGANG: *(Giving a low bow.)* I can, sire.

COURTIER ONE: Let's let him try then.

LEOPOLD: *(To ELECTORATE.)* My lord, this exercise is but a game to Wolfgang, and hardly worthy of presentation before your noble court.

WOLFGANG: But it's fun, Poppa!

ELECTORATE'S WIFE: "Fun?!" How charming!

ELECTORATE: The child is right, Herr Mozart. The carnival season is meant to be filled with games and pleasures of the court.

LEOPOLD: Our only wish is to please, my lord.

ELECTORATE: Then on with it.

(The COURTIERS assemble excitedly around the harpsichord. WOLFGANG is placed a suitable distance away.)

COURTIER TWO: *I* shall play the notes, so that there is no cheating.

WOLFGANG: Pick any you like. I shall know them all.

COURTIER TWO: Shall you indeed? What's this, then? *(Playing a note.)*

WOLFGANG: G.

COURTIER TWO: That was a simple one. Here's another. *(Playing a note.)*

WOLFGANG: B flat, of course.

COURTIER ONE: *(Rushing over, fascinated.)* And this one? *(Choosing a high pitch.)*

WOLFGANG: A. Two octaves above middle C.

COURTIER ONE: How about this? Two at once.

(He plays two notes together.)

WOLFGANG: A C and an F. The interval of a fourth, which is a lovely interval. You can use it along with the pitches you've played in a fascinating improvisation.

(WOLFGANG crosses impulsively to the keyboard.)

COURTIER ONE: Can you indeed.

WOLFGANG: *(Seated at the harpsichord.)* Combine the B flat, the C, and the F, and a pretty melody could come on top, suggested by the G. Like this.

(WOLFGANG combines the notes into an energetic improvisation, which amazes and delights the COURTIERS.)

COURTIER TWO: Extraordinary. How does he think them up so fast?

ELECTORATE'S WIFE: What a perfectly delightful diversion.

(WOLFGANG concludes the piece. The COURTIERS applaud enthusiastically.)

COURTIER ONE: Even *I* am amazed.

WOLFGANG: *(To the ELECTORATE.)* 'Twas fun, wasn't it.

(The COURTIERS laugh with delight.)

ELECTORATE: Why, yes indeed, young man. And for your "fun" I shall see that your father does not return to Salzburg without an expression of our thanks.

LEOPOLD: I am overwhelmed, my lord.

ELECTORATE: Why, it is our pleasure, Herr Mozart. May our payment serve to further this child's promising future.

LEOPOLD: My only wish is that he continue to blossom and grow under my guidance.

ELECTORATE'S WIFE: What a fortunate little boy to have such a devoted father.

LEOPOLD: He is my greatest joy.

COURTIER ONE: Herr Mozart, surely you do not plan to show him off only here in Munich. Why, I should think Vienna is where the child must next perform.

ELECTORATE'S WIFE: Think of the stir he would cause. He would be in great demand as a spectacle at every party.

COURTIER TWO: The rivalry would be fierce to see who gets him first. What "fun!"

ELECTORATE: You realize, Herr Mozart, that before any of the nobility in Vienna can invite you to perform, you must first secure an invitation to perform before the Emperor and Empress.

LEOPOLD: Yes, my lord. I know.

ELECTORATE'S WIFE: That's easy, my dear. Simply write to the Emperor and tell him what a delightful time we've had with these wonder children.

COURTIER TWO: That would no doubt ensure the entrance of the Mozarts into Viennese society.

ANNA MARIA: What a thought!

LEOPOLD: Electorate, your offer is far more generous then we had dared to imagine.

ELECTORATE: Why, it's nothing,

WOLFGANG: No, it's *something!*

(The court chuckles warmly at WOLFGANG's childish outburst.)

LEOPOLD: Again, my son corrects me. Such a letter would, to be sure, make it possible to present the great gifts which my children possess to those who most deserve to hear them.

COURTIER ONE: You are bound to make a success of it. Vienna is the musical capital of the world.

LEOPOLD: May I be successful only in the eyes of God.

COURTIER ONE: Right. Well, that too.

ELECTORATE: You shall no doubt conquer Vienna.

ELECTORATE'S WIFE: Then perhaps a grand tour throughout all of Europe. Such talent mustn't be confined.

LEOPOLD: I shall never confine my children, Madam. My sole ambition is to share God's grace with all who might wish to hear.

ELECTORATE: A generous use of such a gift, Herr Mozart.

LEOPOLD: Thank you, my lord.

(On a cue from LEOPOLD, the Mozart family bows.)

LEOPOLD: And thank you for granting us this performance before your noble court.

2. ANDANTE POCO ALLEGRO

Performance tableau breaks. Mozarts are now in carriage ride home, triumphant. Laughter is heard rising from all of them as scene begins.

WOLFGANG: And what about the fellow before supper who asked—*(In a big pompous voice.)* "Aren't you that amazing little man from Salzburg?"

NANNERL: I'm surprised you didn't say, "No, have you seen him around here somewhere?"

(All laugh.)

WOLFGANG: Well who *else* would I be?

LEOPOLD: *(Teasing.)* Perhaps he thought you were an elf.

WOLFGANG: Poppa!!

NANNERL: Or a goblin.

LEOPOLD: A little musical goblin who goes about casting charms on everyone.

WOLFGANG: *(Grabbing his father playfully.)* A gobliney wobliney—who plays trickzies on Popzy.

LEOPOLD: *(Laughing.)* You'd have to catch me first, my little charmer.

ANNA MARIA: I thought the ballroom was elegant. Did you see all those paintings on the ceiling? Weren't they lovely!

NANNERL: I liked the cherubs on the walls.

WOLFGANG: The little babies with wings flying all over the place? They're silly!

NANNERL: They're sweet!

WOLFGANG: *(Wickedly.)* They're *naked!*

ANNA MARIA: They're angels, Wolferl. Now hush.

WOLFGANG: *(Mimicking the court.)* "I cannot believe that the miracle boy can name every pitch played by every naked angel in the room."

NANNERL: Wolfy!!

WOLFGANG: Naked angels, naked angels!!

LEOPOLD: Wolferl, the nobility may decorate their palaces as they please, no matter how amusing. You mustn't make fun of them.

WOLFGANG: But they're such funny people, Poppa.

LEOPOLD: Truly! But they are also the people who will make it possible for you to be a great musician someday.

ANNA MARIA: They have position in society, darling—

WOLFGANG: And money!

LEOPOLD: And you will need some of it. So, you must learn to impress and not offend the people of wealth and position.

WOLFGANG: *(Playfully slipping back into role.)* "Excuse me, sire. I *don't* mean to offend you, but did you realize that your angels are *naked?*
(ANNA MARIA and NANNERL burst into giggles.)

LEOPOLD: *(Amused.)* You are impossible!

WOLFGANG: Maybe I won't even choose to be a great musician when I grow up.

LEOPOLD: Choose?

WOLFGANG: Maybe I shall be a soldier, or a merchant, or a trader and sail to the South Seas in search of treasure.

LEOPOLD: Why, son. You have been given a great gift of music. God has chosen for you.

NANNERL: I shall be a great musician when I grow up. That's what you would like, isn't it, Father?

WOLFGANG: Always so good, Sissy. Sissy wissy doesy what Popzy wantzy.

ANNA MARIA: Be nice, Wolfy—

NANNERL: I was good tonight, Poppa, wasn't I? The courtiers liked my music, too, didn't they?

LEOPOLD: Of course my dear, you were—

WOLFGANG: *(Interrupting, mimicking.)* "Astounding! Miraculous! What extraordinary children you have, Herr Mozart."

(WOLFGANG hugs his father adoringly.)

LEOPOLD: Thank you, sire. I'm a lucky man to have such a family—silly son and all.

(All laugh and begin to chatter, overlapping as music begins, builds.)

ANNA MARIA: Leopold, did you notice the Electorate's wife's dress? Lovely, wasn't it? And the little cakes after dinner were scrumptious—

NANNERL: *(Overlapping.)* This is so exciting, Poppa. Can we do this some more—

WOLFGANG: *(Overlapping.)* I'll play all night long next time if they want me to, Poppa. It's *fun*—

(A crescendo of music segues into gossip sequence.)

3. MINUET

Four GOSSIPS are engaged in a stately minuet, conversing as they change partners, all the while concealing a romantic intrigue among them.

GOSSIP ONE: Who are these Mozarts anyway? Isn't *she* the daughter of some poorly paid city official?

GOSSIP TWO: And *he* is the son of a bookbinder. He should at least have the decency to be descended from a musical family.

GOSSIP ONE: They are all the same, those musicians. Living off the generosity of the rich.

GOSSIP TWO: Rather than having a *real* profession. The Mozarts have no *real* position in society.

GOSSIP THREE: *(To GOSSIP TWO.)* I heard from a friend of a friend of the Prince-Archbishop Schrattenbach that Leopold Mozart has twice been passed over for the position of Kappelmeister to the Archbishop's court.

GOSSIP TWO: He has been *Vice*-Kappelmeister for years.

GOSSIP THREE: He'll never be promoted now. He spends all of his time teaching his child prodigy.

GOSSIP TWO: I imagine the real reason is that Leopold Mozart is actually a very mediocre composer. He has no hope of *real* success.

GOSSIP THREE: Except for his talented son!

(They laugh.)

GOSSIP FOUR: *(To GOSSIP THREE.)* Have you heard that Leopold Mozart locks his son in a tiny room until he memorizes a new concerto?
GOSSIP THREE: I have heard that he keeps the child there for eight hours—
GOSSIP TWO: For *ten*—
GOSSIP ONE: For *twelve*—
GOSSIP THREE: For *days* at a time!
GOSSIP FOUR: Imagine.

4. IN TEMPO MISURATO

GOSSIPS exit, revealing the Mozart home. LEOPOLD instructs his children in music. WOLFGANG is seated at the harpsichord. LEOPOLD is singing the melody line of the piece that WOLFGANG is practicing. NANNERL is standing by the harpsichord, music in hand, waiting for her turn. ANNA MARIA sits by the window, sewing.

LEOPOLD: *(Singing.)* La dee, la la—stop. Let's build the phrase more, son. It should peak in the fourth measure.
WOLFGANG: Like this?
(WOLFGANG plays and LEOPOLD sings. They complete the phrase.)
LEOPOLD: Yes. Yes!
WOLFGANG: It's like climbing to the top of a stairway, or a mountain!
LEOPOLD: Tell me why, son.
WOLFGANG: Because you *must* reach the top, and when you do it's so wonderful!
LEOPOLD: Exactly! Oh, my precious child.
(NANNERL takes a few steps away from the harpsichord.)
LEOPOLD: Let's go on. See if you can capture the spirit of the next phrase.
WOLFGANG: *(Continuing to play.)* It's so beautiful.
LEOPOLD: Paint a picture—
WOLFGANG: Notes sailing across the sky—
LEOPOLD: To a sense of stillness.
(Father and son sing the final phrase together as WOLFGANG plays the harpsichord. They complete the phrase. LEOPOLD is very moved.)
LEOPOLD: I could listen to you every moment of every day and it still wouldn't be enough.
WOLFGANG: Then, we'll play all night, too, Poppa. Always!
LEOPOLD: Always!
NANNERL: Is it my turn, Poppa?

LEOPOLD: Yes, my dear. Wolfgang, you can accompany your sister.

NANNERL: But Wolferl goes so fast.

LEOPOLD: He shall keep to the beat, won't you, son. Now, ready? One, two, and three. One, two—

(Music. NANNERL begins to sing a sweet song, as LEOPOLD counts the beat. Then WOLFGANG is distracted by a noise outside the window.)

WOLFGANG: Poppa. Look! The market in the square.

LEOPOLD: *(To WOLFGANG.)* My dear—

WOLFGANG: They're setting up so early.

ANNA MARIA: *(Standing to see.)* How lovely!

WOLFGANG: Come see, Sissy. The fruits are more red and more orange than ever before.

(NANNERL moves toward the window, but a look from her father stops her.)

WOLFGANG: Mother, let's go now. Let's not wait till this afternoon.

LEOPOLD: Son, you have several pieces to master before our concert at the Imperial Court in Vienna.

WOLFGANG: But I already know them, Poppa.

LEOPOLD: *(Patiently.)* My dearest child, it is not enough to know a piece. It must be perfect so that the beauty of the music can truly be heard.

WOLFGANG: I want my music always to be heard.

LEOPOLD: Of course you do. That is why we must practice very hard.

(WOLFGANG goes back to the harpsichord.)

LEOPOLD: That's my good child. Ready? One, two, and three. One, two— *(He begins to play.)* Anna Maria, Wolfgang mustn't go to the market this afternoon nor should any such outings be planned before our concert in Vienna. It's too important.

ANNA MARIA: You're not serious—

WOLFGANG: *(Stopping his playing.)* Momma and I always go to the market on Wednesdays.

LEOPOLD: But you would rather stay here and practice with me, wouldn't you, son?

ANNA MARIA: One afternoon away from practicing surely wouldn't matter.

WOLFGANG: And my friends. We always have a game in the square after shopping.

LEOPOLD: I thought music was the most important thing to you, son.

WOLFGANG: It is, Poppa!

NANNERL: Then it is your duty to do what Poppa says.

(WOLFGANG looks to his ANNA MARIA.)

ANNA MARIA: Poppa does make the decisions, Wolferl.

LEOPOLD: They are for your own good—your own best interests.

WOLFGANG: But what if we—

LEOPOLD: Your music, Wolfgang.

WOLFGANG: *(Returning to his harpsichord.)* Yes, Poppa.

(He begins to play again, very intently and very rapidly. NANNERL struggles to keep up with his tempo.)

LEOPOLD: Anna Maria, will you also close the shutters on the window. You know how easily Wolfgang is distracted.

ANNA MARIA: Leopold, now you are being silly. My goodness, the children need sunshine. You can't hope to keep the outside world completely away from them.

(WOLFGANG is playing faster and faster.)

NANNERL: *(Slamming her music book down on the harpsichord in frustration.)* Wolfy!

(WOLFGANG stops playing. All eyes are on NANNERL for her uncharacteristic outburst.)

NANNERL: I'm…sorry, Poppa.

ANNA MARIA: Come then. Let's take a short rest. I think the children have had quite enough practicing for one morning.

(She opens the window. Light floods in.)

WOLFGANG: *(Racing to the window.)* How wonderful.

LEOPOLD: Anna Maria!

NANNERL: Wolferl, come back.

WOLFGANG: Please, Poppa. I won't disappoint you! I'll be so charming before the Emperor and Empress!

(He pulls NANNERL beside him in a quick role-play. He becomes the Emperor.)

WOLFGANG: "What a delightful little wizard this child Mozart is."

NANNERL: *(Enjoying the game.)* "Indeed!"

WOLFGANG: "Why, we shall have to keep him around permanently, for our entertainment."

ANNA MARIA: Wouldn't that be fun, living in the Imperial Palace!

WOLFGANG: *(Hugging LEOPOLD.)* Please, Poppa. I'll be very good and very fun. You said I have a great gift.

LEOPOLD: *(Melting.)* That you do, you little rascal.

WOLFGANG: Let's play a game, Poppa. Just a short one. Then I shall practice for the rest of the day.

NANNERL: Could we, please, Poppa?

ANNA MARIA: Just this once, my dear.

LEOPOLD: *(Easing up.)* All right. Come on.

NANNERL and ANNA MARIA: *(Overlapping.)* Thank you, Poppa. Thank you, dear.

WOLFGANG: *(Arranging everyone in their place in a circle.)* Now, this is my very own game. How you play is that I shall say a letter from the alphabet. Then—you must stand *there*, Nannerl.

NANNERL: All right, bossy.

WOLFGANG: Good! Then I will toss my ball to someone who must say a word beginning with that letter when they catch the ball. Understand?

LEOPOLD: Sounds fun.

ANNA MARIA: You say the word when you catch the ball. Yes?

WOLFGANG: Yes, Momma. Don't be silly, now.

ANNA MARIA: I learned it from you, silly willy.

NANNERL: Throw it to me first, Wolferl.

WOLFGANG: I shall decide! *(He pauses dramatically.)* "D."
    (He throws the ball to NANNERL.)

NANNERL: *(Surprised.)* Dress.

WOLFGANG: Now you say a letter and throw it.

NANNERL: Ah…"S."
    (She throws it to ANNA MARIA.)

ANNA MARIA: Oh goodness, ah…Salzburg. Then…"W."
    (She throws it to WOLFGANG.)

WOLFGANG: Wonderful! "F."
    (He throws it to LEOPOLD.)

LEOPOLD: Flute! "D."
    (He throws it to NANNERL.)

NANNERL: *(Missing the beat.)* Ah…Dragon.

WOLFGANG: You must say the word when you catch the ball, Sissy.

NANNERL: I know.

LEOPOLD: Then count.

NANNERL: "M."
    (She throws it to WOLFGANG.)

WOLFGANG: *(Missing the beat.)* Ah, what's a good one…Mountain!

LEOPOLD: On the beat, Wolfgang. That's what makes it fun. Letter, toss, and word. One, two, and three.
    (LEOPOLD continues to count; "One, two, and three" under the rhythm of the game .)

WOLFGANG: "L." *(He tosses to ANNA MARIA.)*
    (One, two, and…)

ANNA MARIA: Light. "C." *(He tosses to NANNERL.)*
    (Three. One, two, and…)

NANNERL: Crown. "M." *(She tosses to WOLFGANG.)*

(Three. One, two, and...)

WOLFGANG: *(Trying to think of the most wonderful "M" word.)* M...M... *(Three...)*

LEOPOLD: Letter, toss, and word. One, two, and three!

WOLFGANG: *(Breaking out of the circle.)* Please, Poppa. It's only a game. I just want to play!

5. FANTASIA

WOLFGANG runs from the game to his two puppets. Fantasy sequence. He manipulates these two-dimensional jointed puppets in a conversation, echoing the alphabet game.

PUPPET ONE: "M."

PUPPET TWO: Music. "A."

PUPPET ONE: Always. "E."

PUPPET TWO: Everywhere. "L."

PUPPET ONE: Love. "D."

PUPPET TWO: Duty. "P."

PUPPET ONE: Poppa. "W."

PUPPET TWO: Music.

PUPPET ONE: Music?

PUPPET TWO: Yes, music!

PUPPET ONE: "W" is for Wolfgang.

PUPPET TWO: Wolfgang? Who's Wolfgang?

PUPPET ONE: You know him. Music.

PUPPET TWO: Oh *him*!

PUPPET ONE: Well, what is he? A Wolfgang or a music?

PUPPET TWO: Aren't they the same thing?

PUPPET ONE: "W...M"

PUPPET TWO: Wolfgang, music...

WOLFGANG: Music...*Music*...

(The figure of LEOPOLD looms over WOLFGANG. WOLFGANG stiffens, then stands as a puppet, his father manipulating him. With jerky movements, WOLFGANG recites.)

WOLFGANG: "D." Duty. "M" Music. Duty...Music...Music...Duty... Music. *Music!!*

6. ALLEGRO GUISTO

Music is heard. Crescendos. Actors and cutouts assemble as the court of Vienna. WOLFGANG performs the conclusion of a piece brilliantly. He ends to great applause.

FRANCIS I: What a charming little wizard this child Mozart is.

MARIA THERESA: Indeed!

FRANCIS I: Did you enjoy the tour of the royal apartments my children provided for you?

WOLFGANG: Oh yes, your majesty. We've never seen where an Emperor lives before. We saw your bed and everything!

FRANCIS I: Did you, then?

NANNERL: It's all so big.

LEOPOLD: Your children are most generous hosts to my Wolfgang and Nannerl. Never before have we been so warmly welcomed into such a noble home.

COURTIER ONE: And it appears that Young Mozart has plans to remain. The boy slipped upon the marble floor in the palace hall, and little Princess Maria Antonia helped him to his feet. Young Mozart's thanks was a marriage proposal.

FRANCIS I: Marriage, little wizard?

WOLFGANG: Oh yes, your majesty. My father said marrying a princess was the one sure way I could get a royal patron for life.

(The COURTIERS get a good laugh at LEOPOLD's expense.)

COURTIER TWO: A wise little wizard.

LEOPOLD: My son jests, my lord. He is only a child.

COURTIER TWO: Doing just as Poppa says?

COURTIER ONE: You should be more careful, Herr Mozart, that Poppa only pulls the right strings on his little puppet-child.

MARIA THERESA: Nonsense. I'm charmed. Little Mozart is welcome in my home as a suitor to any one of my daughters. He need only ask.

WOLFGANG: *(Runs to MARIA THERESA and hugs her.)* Thank you, Empress.

FRANCIS I: *(Laughing.)* My daughters, yes. My wife, *no!*

ANNA MARIA: He is a very affectionate child, your majesty.

FRANCIS I: And a very gifted one.

COURTIER ONE: One who has been honored with an invitation to perform at Versailles before the King of France?

ANNA MARIA: Isn't it wonderful?!

LEOPOLD: We intend to begin a grand tour in order to reach Versailles by New Year's. Our hope is to perform before every court from Vienna to Paris.

MARIA THERESA: A grand tour! How exciting!

LEOPOLD: Any assistance which your majesties could provide, so that all might share in the glory of my son's music, would be humbly welcomed.

FRANCIS I: I shall be happy to send all the appropriate letters of introduction.

ANNA MARIA: Your Majesty!

MARIA THERESA: It's nothing, my dear. We'll put a court scribe onto it.

LEOPOLD: For your assistance I am most grateful.

COURTIER ONE: I bet you are.

FRANCIS I: Herr Mozart, my imperial paymaster will see that you are handsomely paid for this afternoon's entertainment.

LEOPOLD: With humble thanks, my lord.

FRANCIS I: Our pleasure.

LEOPOLD: And double thanks for contributing to the opportunity to share the miracle of my son's music with the world.

COURTIER ONE: *(Handing LEOPOLD a coin purse.)* Let's not forget the opportunity to make a small fortune off the miracle child as well, eh, Herr Mozart?

LEOPOLD: We take our leave, your highness.

(Mozart family bows on cue. Tableau breaks. Grand tour sequence begins.)

7. ACCELERANDO

THE GRAND TOUR

WOLFGANG and NANNERL are at the harpsichord. Throughout the following sequence there is a whirl of activity around them. BARKERS carry large broadsides announcing WOLFGANG's successes. COURTIERS and INNKEEPERS appear and engage LEOPOLD. ANNA MARIA struggles to keep up with LEOPOLD, pushing the family trunk. Action should be continuous and rapid, music throughout.

BARKER ONE: The greatest wonder in all Germany! Imagine if you can a girl of eleven who plays the most difficult sonatas and concertos—

BARKER TWO: With the most distinct execution, with almost incredible ease, and in the best taste!

LEOPOLD: *(To a COURTIER.)* May I present myself. I am Leopold Mozart, father to the greatest musical wonders in Europe.

COURTIER A: Yes. Your children have quite a reputation, Herr Mozart. The Duke Karl Theodore is most eager to receive you. You may come to the court tomorrow at two.

LEOPOLD: My thanks, sir.

BARKER THREE: Such musical feats alone would be enough to astonish many people. But we are transported with utter amazement when we see a boy of seven years—

BARKER FOUR: Sitting at a harpsichord, and hear him not only playing the same sonatas, trios, and concertos manfully—

BARKER ONE: Not at all like a child!

LEOPOLD: *(To an INNKEEPER.)* My son requires a soft bed, with a warm cover. And make sure that there is an adequate light in the room, for he composes late into the night.

INNKEEPER ONE: Yes, Herr Mozart. Where would you like to have your evening meal?

LEOPOLD: At your best table, in a place where my children can be seen by all who dine at your establishment.

INNKEEPER ONE: We shall have a real crowd tonight then! Lots of folks like to come and just stare at 'em.

BARKER TWO: But also hear the child improvising from his head, for whole hours at a time.

BARKER THREE: Or reading at sight to accompany symphonies—

BARKER FOUR: Arias, and recitative at concerts. Amazing!

LEOPOLD: *(Crossing to WOLFGANG.)* For your amazement, my son will now play the most difficult of concertos without casting a glance at the keyboard. To prove his extraordinary ability, I shall blindfold him. *(Places a blindfold on WOLFGANG.)*

COURTIER B: Look at that!

COURTIER C: And he never says a word!

WOLFGANG: Poppa?

BARKER FOUR: From Augsburg, to Mainz, to Stuttgart, to Frankfurt, the wonder child has dazzled all who have seen him.

BARKER ONE: The child is in great demand.

COURTIER D: *(To LEOPOLD.)* Thank you for your performance, Herr Mozart. As payment, please accept this handkerchief bearing the initials of the Elector Palatine.

LEOPOLD: The Elector sends only this as thanks?

COURTIER D: I should think you'd be pleased, Herr Mozart. The last wandering musicians got a snuffbox!

WOLFGANG: *(Still blindfolded.)* Where are we, Poppa?

NANNERL: This is a concert, Wolferl.

ANNA MARIA: *(To another INNKEEPER.)* My husband has arranged for us to sleep here tonight.

INNKEEPER TWO: Oh yes, madam. And to give a concert after dinner.

ANNA MARIA: A concert? We have given two today already. My children are exhausted!

INNKEEPER TWO: Good money to be made here tonight. I think your husband made a wise choice.

WOLFGANG: *(Still blindfolded.)* Poppa, am I pleasing you?

LEOPOLD: *(To COURTIER E.)* Thank you for your generosity, sir.

NANNERL: Just do as Poppa says, Wolferl.

ANNA MARIA: *(To LEOPOLD.)* Does Wolferl even have a choice?

WOLFGANG: Are you listening, Poppa?

LEOPOLD: *(To COURTIER F.)* It is our pleasure to entertain you, sir.

NANNERL: I'm tired, Momma.

WOLFGANG: The *music*, Sissy!

ANNA MARIA: The children, Leopold!

(Mozart family becomes surrounded by COURTIERS, applauding. Mozart family quickly assumes their performance tableau. Smiles all around, WOLFGANG still blindfolded.)

8. CRESCENDO MOLTO

Performance tableau collapses into the Mozart family, exhausted at a rustic inn, except for WOLFGANG who sits upon the floor busily composing. LEOPOLD is taking inventory of the family's earnings. ANNA MARIA sits resting with NANNERL.

LEOPOLD: Three hundred...Four hundred and fifty-six ducats.

ANNA MARIA: Is that all?

LEOPOLD: We have the handkerchiefs, the jewelry, and the snuffboxes.

ANNA MARIA: Can we not convince our hosts that we would prefer payments of cash?

WOLFGANG: But I love the snuffboxes. They're so tiny and cute.

ANNA MARIA: Tiny, to be sure.

WOLFGANG: And the sword from the Duke in Mannheim. Someday I shall be big enough to carry it.

LEOPOLD: I'm sure you shall, son.

WOLFGANG: And then I'll take all my pretty presents and put them in my palace—a palace just like the Emperor of Vienna's.

ANNA MARIA: That's all very well son. But until that time, you might get hungry with nothing but snuffboxes to eat.

LEOPOLD: Anna Maria—

ANNA MARIA: You know it's true, my dear. This tour is costing us far more than we are earning.

LEOPOLD: We are earning a reputation for Wolfgang! Soon he'll receive commissions from Princes, be offered a well-paying position as a court composer—

ANNA MARIA: The sooner the better, before the poor child collapses from exhaustion. You are pushing him too hard—

LEOPOLD: I want him to be successful.

ANNA MARIA: Let him grow up first. He will be.

NANNERL: Momma, I don't think I want to perform tomorrow. I'd rather just watch.

ANNA MARIA: We'll talk about it, darling. I'm worried about the children, Leopold, and our money. Let's go back to Salzburg at the end of the week.

LEOPOLD: And miss the opportunity to perform before Louis XV of France?

ANNA MARIA: Opportunity for who?

WOLFGANG: *(Not understanding.)* Why for me, of course, Mother.

ANNA MARIA: Yes, of course.

(She begins to unpack the trunk.)

WOLFGANG: I'm not hungry or tired. Are you, Sissy?

NANNERL: Only a little.

WOLFGANG: Besides, the innkeeper will be in soon with our dinner. All the innkeepers love to give us our meals as a present.

ANNA MARIA: Present?

WOLFGANG: Aren't they presents, Poppa? Just like the pretty snuffboxes and the jewelry? The innkeepers let us eat for free, don't they? And sleep, because I am such a good musician?

NANNERL: You're silly, Wolferl.

WOLFGANG: I'm not!

NANNERL: Where have you been? Do you live inside your music all the time?

WOLFGANG: No.

NANNERL: Then do you think this is all magic?

LEOPOLD: That's enough. You children do not need to be concerned with how things are paid for. I want you to think only of your music, Wolfgang.

WOLFGANG: Yes, Poppa.

NANNERL: Me, too, Poppa?

LEOPOLD: We have a concert tomorrow at the Summer Palace of the Wurtemberg Court. If they are generous, we can easily continue our journey to Paris.

ANNA MARIA: Easily? You're as bad as the child, Leopold.

LEOPOLD: I will find the resources somehow. Wolfgang's talents mustn't be wasted.

WOLFGANG: I know what, Poppa. I shall learn to dance. You know how clever I am.

NANNERL: *(Amused.)* Wolfy.

WOLFGANG: And Sissy and I shall perform in the streets and all the people passing by will throw money to us.

(Wolfgang pulls NANNERL to her feet and he pulls her into a dance. He sings while she playfully joins in.)

ANNA MARIA: *(Delighted.)* My little dancing clowns. How precious you are.

WOLFGANG: *(Pulling ANNA MARIA into the dance.)* Momma, you can beat the rhythm on a drumsy wumzy.

NANNERL: Oh yes, Momma.

WOLFGANG: And Poppa, you can—

LEOPOLD: Stop it, Wolfgang. You mustn't be so childish. You're not a monkey in a circus.

(The family stops. A MESSENGER arrives at the door.)

MESSENGER: Mozart?

LEOPOLD: Sir.

MESSENGER: Herr Leopold Mozart?

LEOPOLD: I am he, sir.

MESSENGER: I bring a message from the court of Wurtemberg. The Baron sends his regrets that the entertainments you were scheduled to provide for the court have been canceled for tomorrow. A pheasant hunting expedition has been scheduled in your place.

LEOPOLD: Pheasant hunting?

MESSENGER: According to the Baron's wishes.

LEOPOLD: I see.

MESSENGER: Moreover, he bade me tell you that he does not wish to reschedule the entertainment at this time. He suggests you petition him again after the hunting season.

ANNA MARIA: Thank you, sir.

MESSENGER: *(Exiting.)* I take my leave.

LEOPOLD: So this is how the Mozarts are to be treated? Snubbed by some petty Baron after playing before the Emperor of Vienna!

ANNA MARIA: Leopold—

LEOPOLD: What are we? One of many "diversions" to be selected or thrown away depending on what's in fashion that day?

NANNERL: It's all right, Poppa.

LEOPOLD: Here we are, at the mercy of the whims of the pompous and rich. Hardly even people in their eyes—

WOLFGANG: What's happened, Poppa?

LEOPOLD: We are either petted like animals or given a swift kick out the door like you would a dog that no longer amuses you—

WOLFGANG: Have I done something wrong, Poppa?

LEOPOLD: *(Snapping at WOLFGANG.)* It's not you.

ANNA MARIA: Oh Wolferl—

WOLFGANG: *(Beginning to cry.)* Are you angry at me?

LEOPOLD: No, I'm not angry at you.

WOLFGANG: Why don't they want me, Poppa?

LEOPOLD: It's not you, Wolfgang. It's your music they don't want.

WOLFGANG: But you said I am my music.

(He is crying, confused.)

LEOPOLD: You mustn't think…Oh son…Wolfgang, I promise you that this will never happen again.

ANNA MARIA: Leopold, don't—

LEOPOLD: I vow that you will perform before every monarch in Europe before your next birthday.

WOLFGANG: All right, Poppa.

LEOPOLD: Soon it will be you who is in control. No longer subject to the whims of an ignorant court who couldn't recognize genius if their empty lives depended on it.

ANNA MARIA: You mustn't make him proud.

LEOPOLD: Proud? Yes!

WOLFGANG: I shall no longer play for anyone who cannot recognize my genius. If they are inferior, I shall refuse to play.

LEOPOLD: Wait! You mustn't offend the nobles, son. Merely do not stoop too low. Never loose your dignity.

WOLFGANG: Then I must still please the court?

ANNA MARIA: You're confusing him.

LEOPOLD: You must be perfect.

WOLFGANG: Why?

LEOPOLD: For the sake of your music. Your duty must always be to your music.

WOLFGANG: But I thought my duty was to you, Poppa?

LEOPOLD: *(Holding WOLFGANG to him.)* It is, son. You *must* do as I say. I will guide you all your life so that you can achieve the greatness that God has wished for you.

WOLFGANG: *(Still confused.)* Can we choose another life, Poppa? This one makes you so angry. Just love me, Poppa.

LEOPOLD: Love you? I have sacrificed my career as a composer for you. I have devoted my life to you. Nothing is more precious to me than you! You hold all of my hopes.

WOLFGANG: Who is my music for, Poppa?

LEOPOLD: *(Hugging him.)* For me, son. For *me*.

9. FANTASIA AFFANNATO

Fantasy sequence. WOLFGANG imagines himself surrounded by faceless people, gawking at him. WOLFGANG imagines himself to be a circus barker.

WOLFGANG: Come see the amazing Mozart! The most talented child in the world. He lives in a cage, but he doesn't mind. He does all sorts of wonderful tricks. He plays standing on his head when he plays for the court. He plays with his eyes covered and his ears plugged when he plays for his father. How does he know which way to play? His father tells him. His father tells him *everything*—when to sleep, when to eat, when to walk, when to talk. Don't step outside the cage, little boy. Just obey your father and do everything right. Look at him, Herr Mozart. Isn't he funny? Look at him, look at me. Look at *me!*

(The faceless people [the COURTIERS in mask] surround WOLFGANG throughout the sequence, cutting him off when he reaches out. LEOPOLD remains at a distance, moving in puppetlike motions, bowing to the cutout court, oblivious to WOLFGANG's pleas. On WOLFGANG's final line, the French court enters.)

10. ALLEGRO DI BRAVURA

The KING, QUEEN, and other COURTIERS are assembled about in stiff formality. WOLFGANG is the momentary center of attention. He has the appearance of a slick, accomplished performer, a sort of miniature Courtier.

LOUIS XV: Look at him.

COURTIER ONE: Yes, your majesty.

COURTIER TWO: Immediately, your majesty.

LOUIS XV: He's quite the little Courtier.

COURTIER ONE: Without a doubt, sire.

COURTIER TWO: To be sure.

QUEEN: Precious.

WOLFGANG: *(Bowing low.)* Your majesty.

LEOPOLD: Your majesty, we beg your forgiveness for our late arrival. But the crowds for your day of public audience are immense.

LOUIS XV: I do have enthusiastic subjects. Do I not?

COURTIER ONE: Very loyal, sire.

COURTIER TWO: And very enthusiastic.

LOUIS XV: As I said.

COURTIER TWO: As you most certainly said.

QUEEN: You are four among thousands who have come to catch a glimpse of the King on this New Year's Day.

LEOPOLD: We are very honored to have been so graciously received.

LOUIS XV: Quite. Tell me, little man. Are you the magician of music who so amazed my court yesterday by playing the organ in the Royal Chapel as if you were a full twenty years older and at least a good foot taller?

WOLFGANG: I am, your majesty.

COURTIER ONE: He is.

COURTIER TWO: I should say he is.

WOLFGANG: But your subjects were very easy to amaze, sire.

LOUIS XV: Oh?

QUEEN: Do tell us why, little magician.

WOLFGANG: Because the French know so little about music. Why, one fellow asked if a concerto was a new perfume.

LEOPOLD: *(Trying to divert the King.)* Would your majesty enjoy hearing a minuet which my son has written in your honor?

WOLFGANG: Imagine! After all the beautiful concertos I have played before hundreds of people.

LEOPOLD: *(Grabbing NANNERL.)* Perhaps a piece on the harpsichord for four hands.

WOLFGANG: How could anybody be so stupid. Even if they're French.

COURTIER ONE: What a comment!

COURTIER TWO: Before the King!

LEOPOLD: Sire, I—

LOUIS XV: Charming. This genius of a man in the form of an impulsive child.

COURTIER ONE: Impulsive.

COURTIER TWO: Rude!

LOUIS XV: But you have pleased me and therefore I will allow you the place of honor at our New Year's meal.

LEOPOLD: We are indebted, my lord.

LOUIS XV: Your family will be allowed to take your place—standing behind myself and my Queen as we eat.

COURTIER ONE: No worthier place.

COURTIER TWO: No better perspective on his majesty as he eats.

QUEEN: And you shall be offered whatever we choose not to consume.

LEOPOLD: *(With irony surpressing anger.)* We have never been treated in this manner before, your majesty. I am…amazed.

LOUIS XV: Yes, well, we value the arts in this kingdom, Herr…uhmm…

LEOPOLD: "Mozart."

LOUIS XV: Mozart. No better diversion than a little piece of music.

COURTIER ONE: No better.

COURTIER TWO: Our favorite.

QUEEN: Come, dine with us.

(Stately, boring music begins. The Mozart family takes their place behind the King and Queen. Their conversation is not heard by the court.)

ANNA MARIA: Dining with the King of France.

LEOPOLD: I hope this isn't our only payment.

NANNERL: Look at all this food. How do they eat it all?

ANNA MARIA: They will share it with their subjects, once they have finished, darling.

LEOPOLD: Throw the dogs a bone.

WOLFGANG: Poppa, is this one of the times we are stooping too low or not?

LEOPOLD: *(Caught.)* It must be endured, son.

WOLFGANG: Yes, Poppa.

LEOPOLD: But only endured. In England it will be different.

ANNA MARIA: England? We've only just arrived in France.

LEOPOLD: We leave for England…tomorrow.

(Louis XV court tableau breaks.)

11. ADAGIO NON TANTO

Mozart family now in a boat crossing the English Channel. Each family member has changed. They are not the same family we met in the carriage.

NANNERL: Wolferl, look! The ocean goes as far as you can see. I never imagined it would be so blue.

ANNA MARIA: It is beautiful, isn't it.

LEOPOLD: And our highway to a place where Wolfgang's talents will truly be recognized.

NANNERL: I won't have to perform in London, will I, Momma?

ANNA MARIA: You can choose, my dear.

WOLFGANG: I'm doing everything you ask, aren't I, Poppa?

LEOPOLD: Yes son. You are the perfect child.

NANNERL: Will we get to meet the Queen, Poppa? And to ride across London Bridge?

LEOPOLD: Meeting the Queen is the most important.

ANNA MARIA: Naturally. But I should hope we'll make some time to go to places as a family just for fun.

LEOPOLD: Of course. We shall go to the Opera House so that Wolfgang can hear the Italian operas that are so fashionable in London.

ANNA MARIA: Must everything revolve around music, my dear?

WOLFGANG: Everything does. Right, Poppa?

LEOPOLD: Of course, son. *(To ANNA MARIA.)* You see?

NANNERL: The birds, Wolferl. You aren't noticing the seabirds. They're lovely.

WOLFGANG: May I, Poppa?

LEOPOLD: May you what?

WOLFGANG: Notice the seabirds.

ANNA MARIA: Goodness, Wolferl. You don't need your father's permission to open your eyes. Of course you can look at the birds.

WOLFGANG: I'd like to fly like they do.

LEOPOLD: We all would at this point. How long does it take to get across this channel?

ANNA MARIA: I am feeling a bit odd.

WOLFGANG: *(Looking at the birds.)* They fly so high, so free.

NANNERL: Poppa, can we ask the captain to stop for a minute so the boat will stop rocking?

ANNA MARIA: That won't help, darling. It's the ocean we would have to ask to stop.

(ANNA MARIA and NANNERL, obviously feeling unwell upon the sea, cross away.)

WOLFGANG: *(Looking to his father.)* But the ocean rocks in three-four time, right, Poppa?

LEOPOLD: Yes, Wolferl. In three-four time.

WOLFGANG: *(Conducting the waves.)* One, two, three. One, two, three. One, two, three.

(WOLFGANG rocks with his counting and begins to sing what will become the melody of the second movement of his Symphony No. 4. Preoccupied, LEOPOLD walks away. Segue into the GOSSIP scene.)

12. SCHERZO

BARKER ONE: *One!* Wolfgang Mozart has astounding success in London.

BARKER TWO: *Two!* The greatest triumph of his grand tour.

BARKER THREE: *Three!* Successful concert after successful concert!

(GOSSIPS assemble as if in an opera box, whispering during a concert.)

GOSSIP ONE: King George and Queen Charlotte are charmed by the Mozarts of Salzburg. Have you heard?

GOSSIP TWO: I hear they have been invited before the court *three* times. Every musician in London is very jealous.

GOSSIP ONE: He's only a child after all.

GOSSIP TWO: *(To GOSSIP THREE.)* The child Mozart is the most popular attraction in every London home of any status.

GOSSIP THREE: I have tried to invite him to my house three times but he is always engaged. I don't like to be left out.

GOSSIP TWO: I have an idea as to how we might change the situation.

GOSSIP FOUR: *(To GOSSIP THREE.)* He's a fake!

GOSSIP THREE: Who?

GOSSIP FOUR: Mozart.

GOSSIP THREE: A puppet, I hear.

GOSSIP FOUR: He isn't really a child at all.

GOSSIP THREE: He is a miniature adult.

GOSSIP TWO: With no *real* talents of his own.

GOSSIP THREE: I hear his father is a magician with a music box rigged up inside the harpsichord so that you believe it is really the child playing.

GOSSIP ONE: Shameful!

GOSSIP TWO: What a hoax!

GOSSIP ONE: You know you can visit the Mozart home any day between noon and two o'clock. His father has arranged it.

GOSSIP TWO: So you can see for yourself.

(GOSSIPS' voices have risen in volume throughout.)

OFFSTAGE VOICE: *Shhhhh!!*

(GOSSIPS, highly offended focus their attention back on the concert. Then scene breaks.)

13. ACCELERANDO MOSSO AGITATO

Mozarts are holding court in their London home. Two members of the nobility are just concluding a visitation. LEOPOLD is the master of ceremonies. WOLFGANG sits composing, acknowledging the company only on cue from his father.

NOBILITY ONE: *(Circling WOLFGANG.)* We do appreciate the opportunity to see the child in person.

NOBILITY TWO: You can understand our curiosity.

LEOPOLD: It is our pleasure that we can serve you in this way. Wolfgang loves people.

WOLFGANG: *(On cue.)* Yes, Poppa.

NOBILITY TWO: What a pleasant child. And so obedient.

LEOPOLD: He is very dedicated to his music, madam.

NOBILITY ONE: And to his father, I should think.

NOBILITY TWO: Well I am delighted to learn that he is indeed a child. The rumors are that he is not a child at all, but a dwarf in disguise.

NOBILITY ONE: That he is only a windup doll is what I have heard.

LEOPOLD: It seems that with success comes jealousy from other less talented musicians.

NOBILITY ONE: Or by a baroness who wasn't first in line to display the child at her last party.

LEOPOLD: We try to pay little attention to rumors. Nothing must divert myself or my son in our dedication to music.

NOBILITY TWO: How devoted you are. Thank you, Herr Mozart. *(Exiting.)*

NOBILITY ONE: And all the best for your upcoming concert. I understand that it promises to be quite a success. *(Exiting.)*

LEOPOLD: God has blessed us in England, sir.

ANNA MARIA: *(Entering.)* Who was that Leopold?

LEOPOLD: No one that matters.

ANNA MARIA: I tried to get back, but I needed to get the advertisements for the concert to the gentleman at the Royal Academy.

LEOPOLD: Did you do it?

ANNA MARIA: Yes, I—

LEOPOLD: *(With a singleminded intent.)* Good. And the tickets? Did he say that the fee had been printed clearly on them?

ANNA MARIA: Yes, Leopold. I have done just as you instructed.

LEOPOLD: Excellent.

WOLFGANG: *(Looking up from his composing.)* Poppa?

LEOPOLD: Just a moment, son. And the dress for Nannerl, will it be completed in time?

ANNA MARIA: I was promised it by Friday, as I have told you.

WOLFGANG: Poppa—

LEOPOLD: And the new coat given by King George for Wolfgang?

WOLFGANG: Poppa!

LEOPOLD: Not now, Wolfgang. I need to finalize everything for your concert. There are so many details—

ANNA MARIA: But shouldn't you rest, dear? You were running about town all morning, receiving guests all afternoon. It's not so important.

LEOPOLD: Are you so unaware of how crucial this concert is to us? We stand to earn more money in a single evening than all the evenings spent bowing before the aristocracy combined.

ANNA MARIA: But we have done very well in London, Leopold. Why is this one night keeping you in such a fuss?

WOLFGANG: Poppa—

LEOPOLD: Because every noble in London is clamoring for tickets. Wolfgang is the biggest attraction of London's social season. They are coming to *us* now. And we must astound them. And take them for every pence they are worth.

ANNA MARIA: Honestly, Leopold. I should think you would be more concerned over all the dreadful rumors about Wolferl's abilities. What about his feelings? To think that some people believe that he is only a puppet.

WOLFGANG: *(Bursting in.) Poppa!* I have written a symphony.

LEOPOLD: What?

WOLFGANG: A symphony. Have I pleased you?

LEOPOLD: Son. A complete symphony—

(A visitor arrives. LEOPOLD puts aside the music that WOLFGANG has handed him.)

BARRINGTON: Herr Mozart.

LEOPOLD: Your servant, sir.

BARRINGTON: I realize that the visitations to the child prodigy are scheduled to conclude at two but I imagine you might spare a few moments for me.

ANNA MARIA: *(Clicking into role.)* It is our pleasure to welcome all into our home who desire to see our talented son.

BARRINGTON: So this is the wonder boy.

WOLFGANG: *(Returning to his manuscript.)* Hello.

BARRINGTON: It is an honor, young man.

LEOPOLD: Indeed, I think it is our honor, is it not, sir? Are you not Daines Barrington?

BARRINGTON: I am.

LEOPOLD: Your scholarly writings on music are most impressive, sir.

BARRINGTON: And influential, which is why I am here.

LEOPOLD: Sir?

BARRINGTON: My colleagues at the Royal Academy of Music enjoy a bit of sport. So they have challenged me to administer a test to your son.

ANNA MARIA: A test?

BARRINGTON: To determine scientifically the exact level of his musical skill.

LEOPOLD: For what purpose, sir?

BARRINGTON: The musical establishment requires verifiable proof regarding the child's abilities. How else can we respond to the rumors about town? Some say he is your mechanical toy. Others say that he will write an opera before he is twelve. *(He picks up the music WOLFGANG has been working on.)* Did you write this, little man?
(WOLFGANG nods.)

LEOPOLD: And how would the results of the test be made known?

BARRINGTON: I plan to address the Royal Society of musicians. With my reputation as a musical scholar, my word can hardly be refuted.

LEOPOLD: How perfect.

ANNA MARIA: Mr. Barrington, how would such a test be given?

BARRINGTON: *(Looking at the music, he is astounded.)* I had no idea…Your son would be confined to a room for a full afternoon of performance exercises.

LEOPOLD: Why not extend the examination, sir, to test his skills of composition as well.

BARRINGTON: That would be a rigorous examination, Herr Mozart, lasting three days I should think.

ANNA MARIA: Three days? He is only a child, sir.

LEOPOLD: But three days well spent, proving once and for all that Wolfgang is indeed a child *and* a musical genius.

BARRINGTON: I welcome the challenge, sir.

LEOPOLD: I will make sure that my son is fully prepared to excel in your examination.

ANNA MARIA: Why are you doing this?

BARRINGTON: Because, Madam, I believe your son may have a brilliant future. Possibly more brilliant than any of us can imagine. Unfounded rumors will only stand in his way. Herr Mozart, I will contact you tomorrow to arrange the details.

LEOPOLD: I shall eagerly await them, sir.

BARRINGTON: *(Exiting.)* Farewell.

LEOPOLD: What a perfect opportunity! The final blow to all who are set against the success of my Gala concert. This test will silence them, won't it, son.

ANNA MARIA: Leopold! Are you mad? Why must Wolfgang be subjected to such a test?

LEOPOLD: You just heard why. Don't you understand, or must I explain it to you.

ANNA MARIA: I understand. I understand that Wolfgang no longer matters to you.

LEOPOLD: What?

ANNA MARIA: He *has* become a puppet to you.

LEOPOLD: Don't be absurd.

ANNA MARIA: No. You are the one who is absurd. And wrong! "A test to see if Wolfgang is a child?" You have never let him be a child—always pushing him to live up to your dreams.

LEOPOLD: Of course they are my dreams, just as they are his. Wolfgang's only desire is to be a great musician.

ANNA MARIA: It is your desire! Admit to that at least.

LEOPOLD: I have always made decisions in his best interest—

ANNA MARIA: *Your* interest! To win a place in a society where we don't belong.

LEOPOLD: What's this? You are the one who was always so impressed by the glitter of the court.

ANNA MARIA: Of course I was. But I was content to dream of dressing like an Empress someday. You are using our child to prove something—something to a group of people whom you despise.

LEOPOLD: I haven't used him. I gave Wolfgang choices all along the way.

ANNA MARIA: Choices? Wolfgang doesn't know what the word means, do you?

(Wolfgang remains silent.)

ANNA MARIA: You have made every decision of his life for him. A child? He'll probaby remain a child all his life because of the way you have treated him. He's helpless.

LEOPOLD: He will always be in my care!

ANNA MARIA: I am sure he will. Playing out your ambitions at his expense. Do you ever consider if Wolfgang is happy?

LEOPOLD: Happy? He is brilliant!

ANNA MARIA: And that is all that matters?

LEOPOLD: His music is what matters! Wolfgang is his music!

ANNA MARIA: Oh Leopold, no. He is so much more. You don't see it anymore. I've watched it happen. Every day he slips further away from you. He needs you…just to be his Poppa.

LEOPOLD: He is undisciplined, impulsive. His music will be lost if I am not in control of him.

ANNA MARIA: So you would rather lose your son?

LEOPOLD: He is devoted to me!

ANNA MARIA: What choice does he have?

LEOPOLD: I must choose for him. He's not like other children.

ANNA MARIA: Of course he is.

LEOPOLD: He is a genius.

ANNA MARIA: He is your *son!*

(Their voices crescendo. WOLFGANG, who has been sitting silently during the argument, runs to his puppets.)

14. FANTASIA PATETICO

A fantasy sequence. WOLFGANG manipulates his puppets as MR. and MRS. MUSIC.

MR. MUSIC: I'd like you to meet our son Wolfgang.

MRS. MUSIC: He was born with a harpsichord for a body, a violin for a head, and organ pedals for feet.

WOLFGANG: "How very lucky you are, Mr. and Mrs. Music. And how very lucky your son is." *No! (WOLFGANG hurls his puppets to the ground.)* I'm not just you. I am not just music. I hate you. You have made me different. Alone. I am *not* only music…I'm…I'm…

(LEOPOLD's figure looms in the distance. His father's voice swells, unrelentingly. WOLFGANG is surrounded by the COURTIERS and the cutouts. He tries to break out.)

LEOPOLD'S VOICE: You will be the most famous child in all of history and the greatest composer of all time…the most famous child in history…the greatest composer of all time…the most famous child…the most famous child—

WOLFGANG: *(Reaching out.)* Poppa! Come back!

(The music becomes a collage of pieces that WOLFGANG will write. It is as if he is hearing his future. He turns and listens, completely consumed, as the COURTIERS disappear.)

15. RALLENTANDO

WOLFGANG's fantasy is broken by the entrance of his sister. He is dazed.

NANNERL: Wolferl? Wolfy!

WOLFGANG: What?

NANNERL: Wolfy!

WOLFGANG: Poppa?

NANNERL: It's Nannerl, silly.

WOLFGANG: Oh.

NANNERL: Come play in the garden with me.

WOLFGANG: What does Poppa say?

NANNERL: He's not here. But Mother says that we should go outside to play. You can make friends with the children who live in the next house.

WOLFGANG: Children?

NANNERL: They're very nice. They have two kittens and they want us to go to St. James Park with them so we can feed the ducks. It'll be fun.

WOLFGANG: What would I say to them, Nannerl?

NANNERL: Silly! You are always very funny and charming to Poppa's friends, and especially before the nobles.

WOLFGANG: Other children?

NANNERL: Yes! I spend all my afternoons with them. They're nice.

WOLFGANG: Children?

NANNERL: When you are finished being silly, Wolferl, you can come out into the garden where you belong. I'll wait for you.

(NANNERL begins to leave. She stops, turns, and looks at her brother, then exits. WOLFGANG is drawn like a magnet back to his music, which is scattered on the floor. He gathers it up and clutches it to him, long and hard.)

WOLFGANG: *(To his music.)* Here. Here is where I belong.

(With complete focus, WOLFGANG begins composing furiously. Music, as if in his head, grows and grows. This music segues into a bravado performance of a chamber piece conducted by WOLFGANG from the clavier. Cutouts and actors assemble in the most glittering configuration yet. WOLFGANG is at the peak of his showmanship. The piece concludes to great applause.)

16. FINALE

WOLFGANG is surrounded by adoring fans after his London Gala. ANNA MARIA and NANNERL are present. WOLFGANG is engaging the COURTIERS in a game. He is in complete control.

COURTIER ONE: Congratulations, Herr Mozart. Your concert is a smashing success.

COURTIER TWO: Never before have I seen London so turned on its ear by a musician.

COURTIER ONE: You have much to be proud of, "Leopold."

LEOPOLD: It is an important day for us.

COURTIER TWO: Indeed it is. What with the results of the Barrington test being announced today as well.

COURTIER ONE: I was astounded by the results!

LEOPOLD: You are not alone, sir.

COURTIER TWO: To think that your son is already more gifted than many musicians ever become in their lifetime!

COURTIER ONE: And it appears to all come so naturally to him. Or do you really keep him chained to the harpsichord, Leopold? *(Laughing.)*

COURTIER THREE: Herr Mozart.

LEOPOLD: Sir?

COURTIER THREE: I know it's early to say, but the receipts from the concert suggest that this evening will prove most profitable, sir.

LEOPOLD: I had no doubt that it would.

COURTIER THREE: Congratulations. Tonight you have truly triumphed.

LEOPOLD: My thanks, sir. *(To ANNA MARIA.)* Anna Maria?
(She crosses to him.)
LEOPOLD: There are two important gentlemen here tonight I need you to meet.
ANNA MARIA: What do you want from them?
LEOPOLD: An invitation to perform at the Court of St. James for the upcoming Festival.
ANNA MARIA: All right. In half an hour, I shall be taking the children home.
LEOPOLD: What?
ANNA MARIA: They have fulfilled their duty to you tonight. Wolfgang needs rest.
LEOPOLD: Come, my dear. Don't rob Wolfgang of his greatest night of glory.
ANNA MARIA: His?
(She crosses away.)
COURTIER ONE: *(Passing by.)* What a tribute to you tonight, Herr Mozart.
COURTIER TWO: *(Passing by.)* A more brilliant teacher never lived.
PUBLISHER: Leopold?
LEOPOLD: Karl. What a pleasure.
PUBLISHER: *(Taking LEOPOLD aside.)* You didn't think I would lose the chance to sell a few of your child's compositions by missing the Gala tonight.
LEOPOLD: You publishers have a keen eye for business.
PUBLISHER: You should be glad I have. My decision to publish Wolfgang's six Sonatas was a wise one.
LEOPOLD: How so?
PUBLISHER: They have been so successful that the profits will enable us to publish the manuscript of the child's first symphony before the end of the year.
LEOPOLD: Just in time for the court's end of year celebrations—
PUBLISHER: Which always require a new symphony to add to the festivities.
LEOPOLD: Excellent, Karl.
PUBLISHER: I have already begun to print the second movement, which is, as I am sure you know, dedicated to you.
LEOPOLD: I am ashamed to admit that I have not even seen the composition. The preparations for this evening's concert have absolutely consumed me.
PUBLISHER: Rightly so. But I have brought along a copy. I thought it might be the crowning glory of a successful evening.
LEOPOLD: *(Taking the manuscript.)* Thank you.
(The publisher goes back into the festivities. LEOPOLD pauses a moment. He opens the manuscript and reads.)

LEOPOLD: "Dedicated dutifully to my father."

(LEOPOLD turns the pages of music. The sound of the crowd celebrating fades as the music of second movement of his Symphony No. 4 is heard. All noise goes away, except for WOLFGANG's new composition, which is distinctly new in sound—more beautiful. Sheer perfection.)

LEOPOLD: Oh, my son. *(He begins to weep silently.)* My child, I have been forgetting to listen. Forgive me. Forgive me—

(LEOPOLD closes the manuscript. The sounds of the crowd celebrating return. LEOPOLD tries to make his way across the crowd to his son, but cutouts and characters cut him off each time he tries.)

COURTIER ONE: How proud you must be, Herr Mozart.

COURTIER TWO: How does it feel to be the father of the most famous child in all of Europe?

LEOPOLD: Wolfgang!

COURTIER THREE: The most famous child who ever lived?

COURTIER TWO: You'd best hold on to him, Herr Mozart. He'll soon belong to history.

COURTIER ONE: He won't be your child forever.

LEOPOLD: Wolferl!

(The crowd stops. All eyes are on LEOPOLD. WOLFGANG steps outside of a circle of admirers. He stands across from his father.)

WOLFGANG: Have I displeased you, Father?

(A long pause.)

LEOPOLD: No.

WOLFGANG: Because tonight, Father, you have won.

(They stand silently looking at one another. Neither can reach across the space that separates them. Instead, WOLFGANG turns away from his father and begins to repeat his father's words, addressing both the assembled crowd of the concert and the audience.)

WOLFGANG: I will be the greatest composer of all time.

LEOPOLD: Son. Come back.

WOLFGANG: I will live forever through my music. *(WOLFGANG is surrounded by actors and cutouts, silently applauding, encircling him, cutting him off from his father.)* I am *Mozart.*

(Explosion of applause. LEOPOLD watches silently as WOLFGANG exits with the COURTIERS through the upstage doors. The doors close.)

FINITO

Dancing Solo

FOR MY UNCLE

Photograph from the poster for the original production of Dancing Solo,
MUNY/Student Theatre Project, St. Louis, Missouri, 1991.
Photo: Meoli/Lohbeck Studios, Advertising Agency: Glannon & Company.

ORIGINAL PRODUCTION

Dancing Solo was commissioned and first presented by the MUNY/Student Theatre Project in St. Louis, Missouri, on January 11, 1991. The production was directed by Mary Hall Surface, choreography by Jan Feager, set by Darren Thompson, costume design by Gail Kincaid, property design by Amy Allen, sound design by David Medly and Mary Hall Surface. The company manager was Kenny Jacobs. The producer was Larry Pressgrove. The project was initiated by Bill Freimuth. The cast was as follows:

KARA . . . . Pamela Nowak
DAVID . . . . Robert A. Mitchell
CARLIE . . . . Michelle Muriel
JAKE . . . . Paul Tomak
MELODY . . . . Tonya Dixon

Dancing Solo was underwritten by a generous grant from the Monsanto Fund. Research and assistance was provided by the National Council on Alcoholism and Drug Abuse, St. Louis Area.

CHARACTERS

KARA ROBERTS: Sixteen years old, high school junior, an accomplished modern dancer

DAVID BROTHERS: Late twenties, Kara's dance coach

JAKE REYNOLDS: Seventeen years old, a high school senior, Kara's boyfriend

MELODY LAMPLEY: Sixteen years old, a high school junior, Kara's best friend

CARLIE ROBERTS: Thirty-eight years old, Kara's mother

SETTING

The set should suggest a dance studio—a series of freestanding dance bars, two stools and three upstage frames to represent the mirrored walls of the studio. The action of the play, in real time, takes place in David's dance studio. But Kara's attempt to choreograph her dance is also the physicalization of her internal struggle to understand and control her life. The scenes between David and Kara must work theatrically on two levels. David is watching and reacting to the dance that Kara is rehearsing. But Kara, through her dance, is also confronting memories, as well as immediate present realities, as she struggles to find "the steps" she wants to take.

All settings for the memory and future scenes are created by rearranging the positions of the dance bars and stools. This nonrealistic scenery and only minimal props are essential to the style and flow of the play.

Music for the original production was chosen from piano music of Erik Satie, Claude Debussey, Samuel Barber and others. Underscoring for the future fantasy sequences was composed on electronic instruments.

MUSIC up. The Set is the interior of a Dance Studio. DAVID, a dance teacher, enters. He is impatient, pacing. KARA enters. She is sixteen-years-old and dressed in a dance leotard, tights, and leg warmers. She rushes into the studio, tossing her backpack into a corner. She looks at DAVID, then backs away from him. DAVID turns away. [He remains frozen throughout the following sequence.]

KARA begins a modern dance that reveals her present emotional turmoil. Her first steps are a series of balance moves. But as she shifts her weight from one side to the other, she loses her equilibrium. Frustrated, she begins again, but her moves become quicker, sharper, as if her body is being pulled in directions she does not want to go. The dance becomes more and more frenetic.

JAKE: *(Appearing in one of the upstage mirror-frames. He is a voice, a memory, inside of KARA's mind.)* Just do it for me, Kara.
(KARA dances toward the voice.)
JAKE: Please. Just make the call. Just this once. I need you!
(KARA breaks away from the memory of JAKE, but dances into another memory.)
CARLIE: *(Appearing in one of the upstage mirror-frames.)* Just this once, honey. It won't happen again. I promise.
(KARA spins away from CARLIE as fast as she can, but she is confronted by yet another voice.)
MELODY: *(Appearing in one of the upstage mirror-frames.)* You promised! I can't believe you!
(KARA reaches out for MELODY, but "MELODY" turns away. KARA is then bombarded by all of the memories—a rush of words. She spins from one to the other. Her dance is completely out of control.)
JAKE: Trust me, Kara.
CARLIE: *(Overlapping.)* Don't you trust me?
MELODY: *(Overlapping.)* I trusted you.
JAKE: *(Overlapping.)* I promise.
CARLIE: *(Overlapping.)* It's our secret.
MELODY: *(Overlapping.)* You promised!
CARLIE: *(Topping all the other voices.)* Don't ever tell *anyone!*
(KARA's dance halts. MUSIC stops. The memories vanish. KARA is warming up at the bar for her dance class.)
DAVID: You're late.
KARA: I'm sorry.

DAVID: We don't have to be here, Kara.

KARA: Yes we do.

DAVID: Are you committed to finishing this?

KARA: Of course I am. I'm sorry.

DAVID: Stop apologizing.

KARA: *(Apologizing for apologizing.)* Sorry.

DAVID: Kara!

KARA: Can we just get started? *(She begins to do a series of vigorous dance warm-ups.)* Here I am. Your prize pupil. Ready to dance. *(She loses her balance.)*

DAVID: Kara, what's wrong.

KARA: *(Resuming.)* Nothing.

DAVID: I don't think you can work like this.

KARA: Like what? I'm fine. *(She stops her warm-ups.)* A phone. There's a phone here, isn't there?

DAVID: You need it?

KARA: I...might.

(KARA resumes her warm-ups, but she is not focused.)

DAVID: You are *really* distracted. Let's forget today's lesson, OK?

KARA: No.

DAVID: The audition's a month away. *(DAVID starts to leave.)* But don't forget, the application is due tomorrow.

KARA: Tomorrow...God...David, stop!

(He does.)

KARA: I...*(Regaining control.)* I've got to work on this audition. You want me to get into the summer dance program, right?

DAVID: Then why were you late?

(KARA is still and silent.)

DAVID: Kara—

KARA: My dance!

DAVID: You want to finish it?

KARA: Yes.

DAVID: Then finish it!

KARA: I don't know how!

DAVID: Ask me to help you.

KARA: *(She looks at DAVID, differently, for an instant, then looks away.)* I just want all the parts to *fit.*

DAVID: It's up to you. You're the one setting the moves.

(KARA tries to sketch through several sequences of her dance.)

DAVID: You've already set the beginning, and the middle—

KARA: But not the end!

DAVID: What do you want the dance to say? Work from the inside, find what you feel—

KARA: *(Repeating DAVID's words with him, a remembered mantra.)* Find what you feel—

DAVID: —and dance it!

KARA: *(Stopping.)* I don't know what I feel. I don't know the steps, the moves—

DAVID: Let me help! I know you can do this. You're pretty amazing when you wanna be.

(KARA smiles at DAVID.)

DAVID: Let's work on the end.

KARA: Can't I just repeat a pattern I know?

DAVID: Is that the story you want to tell?

KARA: It was easier at the beginning. Can we start there?

DAVID: Let's review.

(KARA stands still. She begins to focus. MUSIC up softly.)

DAVID: Make sure you're centered. Breathe.

(A kind of shiver runs through KARA.)

DAVID: You're sure you're OK?

KARA: Let me dance it.

(Music in. KARA begins a very lovely dance sequence, that flows lyrically from one move to the next. It is filled with graceful extensions and soft lines. All is in balance. [Throughout the dance sequences KARA is speaking to herself.])

KARA: The beginning. It was perfect.

DAVID: *(Coaching.)* That's it. Reach. Reach!

KARA: *(Dancing.)* I want to. I did.

DAVID: Beyond yourself.

(DAVID shifts the dance bars into a new configuration.)

KARA: *(Dancing.)* For Melody.

(MELODY enters.)

KARA: My best friend. It was all so great, so right.

(KARA remembers when MELODY came to KARA's job at the pizza parlor. As MELODY speaks, KARA crosses into the scene. MUSIC out.)

MELODY: One medium, thick-crust, deep-dish—

KARA: Melody!

MELODY: Pepperoni and mushroom to go.

KARA: Melody! I'm not on break yet. You want me to get in trouble with the manager?

MELODY: Thought you got a break at 6:30?

KARA: 6:35!

MELODY: Five minutes don't matter to a bunch of pepperonis. Come on!

KARA: The manager is not a pepperoni. He's big and he yells, OK?

MELODY: How do you stand bein' around dead pizza crusts all night?

KARA: Don't start—

MELODY: And wiping up all the nasty cheese and olives slopped all over the salad bar!

KARA: You know how much the summer dance program costs?

MELODY: You're the dancer, girlfriend. I'm a photographer. Shootin' stills of life—

KARA: Two hundred dollars! If you needed that kind of money, bet you'd swing spaghetti, too.

MELODY: Haven't you earned that yet, Super-waitress, just in tips?

KARA: I wish!

MELODY: It's 6:31!

KARA: That means you've only got four more minutes to hang out.

MELODY: *(Teasing her.)* Guess you'll just have to wait to hear the good news.

KARA: What?

MELODY: Oh nothing. It's just about Jake.

KARA: Jake?!

MELODY: Um-hum.

KARA: What about him? Melody!

MELODY: *(Lips sealed.)* Gotta wait. It's only 6:32. *(Counting out seconds calmly.)* And twenty-seven, twenty-eight—

KARA: *(Calling to her boss.)* Clocking out for fifteen!

(The girls race away from the work area, and perch upon two stools to talk.)

KARA: What happened? Did it work? Can he come?

MELODY: Well. Dorien called me after school—

KARA: Like he does *every day!*

MELODY: I got this boyfriend trained! Anyway, he said that Jake told his father that he *had* to go to the party tonight. It's an "official track team function." Wouldn't want to disappoint the coach.

KARA: Well, that is sort of true. The party *is* at Jeff's house—

MELODY: And Jeff *is* the captain of the track team.

KARA: *Who cares!* He's coming! I'm gonna die, Melody.

MELODY: Don't you let Jake smoke anything, Kara, or he'll end up grounded again.

KARA: Jake just got stupid last weekend. He was acting out a dare by some guy—I don't know. He promised it was a one-time thing. God, I look awful. I gotta get home and change!

MELODY: There's gonna be dancin'—

KARA: What am I gonna wear?

MELODY: And there's a huge backyard, with big beautiful trees—

KARA: Oh, God—

MELODY: Where you can sit under the stars and "talk!"

(The girls explode with delighted laughter, anticipating what is to come.)

KARA: I still can't believe it's true. Jake Reynolds actually wants to be with *me.*

MELODY: Well, I don't know if he's comin' to be with *you* or not—

KARA: What? What did he say?!

MELODY: I'm kidding. I'm kidding.

(The girls laugh.)

MELODY: Girl, you are *nuts* about this guy.

KARA: It's just all so new.

MELODY: Isn't it great? That's when every word, every look is so…important.

KARA: You say it so right, Melody.

MELODY: You can almost touch what's happening between you.

KARA: I wanna hold onto it forever. I don't want it to ever go away.

MELODY: And we are talkin' a full moon tonight, girlfriend.

KARA: It'll be perfect. You and Dorien.

MELODY: And you and Jake.

(MUSIC in. MELODY exits as KARA resumes her beautiful dance.)

DAVID: Good!

KARA: *(Dancing.)* It *was* good. The party. It was perfect.

DAVID: Lift.

KARA: *(Dancing.)* He came to be with me. Just me.

(Music out. KARA completes the final dance move of this sequence and holds it.)

DAVID: Release.

(KARA releases from the final move. She is very up. "Remembering" the beginning has energized her.)

DAVID: Now, *that's* my prize pupil.

KARA: Let's go to the next beat. It feels so good to remember.

DAVID: OK. Next beat.

KARA: The next week.

DAVID: Tell the story.

(CONCERT MUSIC in.)

KARA: The concert. I soared so high!

(KARA remembers the concert at school where she performed. MELODY and JAKE enter, as if in the audience along with DAVID. The three applaud KARA, who completes an impressive series of moves.)

MELODY: That's my best friend up there!

DAVID: Bravo, Kara!

JAKE: Awesome!

(CONCERT MUSIC out. All cheer and applaud as KARA bows. Then KARA becomes still, remembering that moment.)

KARA: Everyone applauding. All looking at me. Everyone…Mom? *(Looking for her Mother.)* Mom!

(MELODY and DAVID exit. KARA remembers being backstage, immediately after the concert.)

JAKE: Kara?

KARA: Jake! Hi!

JAKE: You were terrific.

KARA: No I wasn't.

JAKE: What do you mean? The whole school was applauding like crazy. I didn't know you could dance like that.

KARA: Like what?

JAKE: Like…so…good. *(He swings her around playfully.)* Hey, I mean, we tore up the rug at Jeff's party, but today, you looked like a dancer on TV. In a ballet or something.

KARA: It's not really ballet. I do modern dance.

JAKE: Oh. Hey, you're gonna have to teach me about dance. I wanna know everything.

KARA: No you don't.

JAKE: Kara, why would I say I do if I don't?

KARA: I don't know.

JAKE: I wanna know everything about you.

KARA: There's not much to know.

JAKE: I don't believe that.

KARA: It's true.

JAKE: You're like nobody else.

KARA: *(Giggling.)* I'm not.

JAKE: So, Ms. Prima Ballerina, may I have the pleasure of your super-talented company for dinner this evening?

KARA: I told my Mom I'd be home tonight—

JAKE: Come on! We gotta celebrate your concert—how great you were. I wanna celebrate us, too.

(KARA melts.)

JAKE: What's your favorite restaurant? Where d' you wanna go?

KARA: I don't have a favorite.

JAKE: How 'bout O'Conners.

KARA: Jake! That's too expensive.

JAKE: For you, nothing is too expensive. (Pause.) I *want* to take you there. OK?

KARA: (Smiling.) OK.

JAKE: Pick you up at seven?

KARA: That's perfect.

JAKE: Great.

(He begins to leave.)

KARA: Jake? Can you pick me up at Melody's? I'll be over there after school.

JAKE: I always pick you up over there. You two livin' together or somethin'?

KARA: She's my best friend.

JAKE: Someday I'm comin' to *your* house. I gotta see where a famous dancer lives.

KARA: Someday.

JAKE: You're mysterious. I like that.

KARA: You do?

JAKE: You're magic. (He exits.)

(MUSIC in. KARA's dance begins again. Her moves are quick and light, almost flighty, as she springs with excitement about her romance.)

KARA: (Dancing.) "Magic." Jake saw me. He saw me dance.

DAVID: Every movement—

KARA: (Dancing.) Is for him.

DAVID: —must build on the one before it.

KARA and DAVID: (Dancing.) Like a poem—

DAVID: It's part of a whole.

KARA: I'm dancing for you, Jake.

(KARA is suddenly still, posed, reaching, her arms outstretched.)

KARA: I need someone to dance for. I'm dancing for you!

(CARLIE enters.)

CARLIE: Kara.

(KARA quickly pulls her arms back toward her body. KARA remembers coming home from school, several days after the concert. MUSIC out.)

KARA: Mom. You're home. It's only 3:30.

CARLIE: I left my desk-insanity behind a bit early today. I'm not feeling well.

KARA: Things still crazy at work?

CARLIE: The usual. A phone that never stops ringing and a boss who expects you to leap through hoops of fire at least three times a day.

KARA: You want anything to eat? I was gonna make a sandwich.

CARLIE: No honey. You go ahead. I'll have a bite later.

KARA: Iced tea or something?

CARLIE: I'd prefer the something.

KARA: Mom—

CARLIE: Anything new and wonderful at school?

KARA: Things are OK.

CARLIE: Grades?

KARA: The quarter doesn't end for a few weeks. We get grades then.

CARLIE: I thought you just got grades?

KARA: That was a couple of months ago.

CARLIE: How time flies when you're chained to a mail-order desk. Well, I'm sure you'll do fine, sweetheart. You always do just fine.

KARA: I did have a concert.

CARLIE: You did? When?

KARA: Last Friday. It went really well.

CARLIE: Why didn't you tell me about it?

KARA: I did.

CARLIE: Why didn't you remind me then?

KARA: I did. On Thursday.

CARLIE: You must have forgotten to remind me. Because I would have remembered. I love to see you dance. Why, I remember when you got your first little pink tights—

KARA: *(Joining in, since this story is told so often.)* "Little pink tights—" Mom, you sure you don't want something to eat?

CARLIE: Why didn't you tell me you had a concert?!

KARA: I *did*, Mom. You just forgot. *(Under her breath.)* Just like the last time.

CARLIE: What did you day?

KARA: Nothing.

CARLIE: I don't like mumbling.

KARA: Sorry.

CARLIE: I don't need you mumbling around me.

KARA: And I don't need you blaming me for something that isn't my fault. I didn't forget to remind you. You didn't remember to come.

CARLIE: *(Hurt.)* I see. Well. I love to see you dance. I'll have to come next time, if you still want me to.

KARA: Of course I do. I'm sorry—

CARLIE: I never want to disappoint you, honey.

KARA: I know.

CARLIE: It's this job. I can't stand it. It's so stupid—so meaningless.

KARA: It's not—

CARLIE: Sitting there day after day. Writing down orders for all these beautiful things then packing them up in big brown boxes and mailing them off to somebody else. It's cruel.

KARA: I'll get you something beautiful, Mom. You name it.

CARLIE: Ummm, anything?

KARA: Anything.

CARLIE: How about a villa in the south of France.

KARA: *(In a playful French accent.)* With or without a handsome Frenchman?

CARLIE: Oh with. Definitely with. As long as he's rich.

KARA: He'd have to be rich to come with a villa.

CARLIE: That sounds so wonderful! But right now, I'll settle for a sandwich.

KARA: You got it. Ham and cheese?

CARLIE: Oh, a delicacy to be sure. And bring me a beer, please sweetheart, OK?

KARA: OK.

> *(MUSIC in. The music is dissonant—the rhythm is irregular, unpredictable. CARLIE exits. KARA begins to dance again, trying to execute a series of identical, controlled turns, but the music challenges her—throws her off.)*

DAVID: What happened?

KARA: *(Dancing.)* The rhythm changed.

DAVID: Can't you follow it?

KARA: *(Dancing.)* How I am supposed to follow it? I never know what's going to happen next.

DAVID: Didn't you choose the music?

KARA: *(Dancing.)* No! I didn't choose it. And I can't change it.

DAVID: Then change the dance.

KARA: *(She stumbles.)* Crazy, stupid, unpredictable music!

DAVID: Change the dance. Make it fit.

KARA: *(Pacing, not dancing.)* I want it to fit. I *hate* it when it falls apart.

DAVID: When is it beautiful? When does it work?

KARA: *Never!* No…sometimes.

> *(The music changes, it is more melodic and calm.)*

KARA: Sometimes everything seems fine. *(KARA begins to dance again. Her body relaxes into the certainty of the rhythm.)* To flow…to be so beautiful.

DAVID: Dance it.

(KARA enjoys this sequence for a few more phrases. Then she remembers the night of her sixteenth birthday. CARLIE enters. MUSIC out.)

CARLIE: How's the birthday girl?

KARA: Hungry.

CARLIE: So, dinner is a little late. I have cooked you the most amazing meal. Every one of your favorites.

KARA: You shouldn't have done all this, Mom.

CARLIE: And why not? You only turn sweet sixteen once in your life. *(Singing.)* "Six-teen candles!"

(CARLIE twirls KARA around in a 50s dance move.)

KARA: *(Laughing.)* You're crazy!

CARLIE: *(Singing.)* "On a sweet cake of white. Shining so bright—"

KARA: You're making up the words!

CARLIE: So? I'm being creative. *(Singing.)* "Burnin' all night, feelin' just right."

KARA: I love you.

CARLIE: Aren't you a sweetheart. Now, every girl should toast her sixteenth birthday with a little bubbly. *(CARLIE offers KARA a glass.)* Here, baby.

KARA: Mom—

CARLIE: Just one glass. That's *all* I'll let you have.

KARA: How many have you had?

CARLIE: *(Sweetly.)* It's not polite to ask.

KARA: I don't want to have alcohol-breath.

CARLIE: Kara! This is not "alcohol!" This is champagne! The drink of elegance, of sophistication. Here, a toast! *(In their playful French accent.)* To our villa *en France!*

(KARA takes the glass from her Mother.)

CARLIE: May all your dreams come true, honey. Now make a wish! No, wait. That's for blowing out birthday candles, isn't it. Oh, make a wish anyway.

KARA: Can I keep it secret?

CARLIE: You *have* to keep it secret. That's the only way wishes come true.

KARA and CARLIE: Cheers.

(They clink glasses. KARA takes a sip.)

CARLIE: So what d'you wish?

KARA: Mom!

(KARA puts her glass down.)

CARLIE: I know, I know. Can't trust me with a secret. Can't trust me with anything.

KARA: So what's for dinner? It smells wonderful.

CARLIE: Out of the kitchen.

KARA: But I'm starving.

CARLIE: You in a hurry to rush off somewhere?

KARA: No. It's just…It's eight o'clock, and you said we'd eat at 6:30 and I told Jake—

CARLIE: Just one more glass, then our birthday banquet will begin.

KARA: Can I at least take everything out of the oven?

CARLIE: Don't you want to sit and talk with your Mother? *(She pours another glass.)* I thought that's what tonight was all about? A nice, leisurely evening together.

KARA: Please don't have any more.

CARLIE: We're celebrating, honey. This champagne is in *your* honor.
(Doorbell sounds.)

CARLIE: Ooo, a mystery guest.

KARA: I'll go.

CARLIE: I'll have to get another glass.

KARA: Mom!
(JAKE appears at the door.)

KARA: Jake!

JAKE: Surprise! *(He hands KARA a rose.)* For you. Almost as pretty as you are.

CARLIE: Why a gentleman caller! Come in!

JAKE: Thanks.

CARLIE: Kara, you stinker. You didn't tell me you'd invited this nice young man to our party.

JAKE: I surprised her, Mrs. Roberts. *(To KARA.)* Been waitin' for you. Don't you wanna go to Twists? You know, go dancin' on your birthday? *(To both.)* I didn't mean to interrupt anything.

CARLIE: Not at all! So introduce us, Kara.

KARA: This is Jake Reynolds, Mom.

JAKE: Nice to meet you.

CARLIE: I've been wondering when Kara was finally going to let me meet this boy who has her heart turned upside down.

KARA: Mom!

CARLIE: Well, it's true, isn't it?
(Both teenagers smile, embarrassed.)

CARLIE: Oh why is romance wasted on the young.

KARA: The rose is beautiful. Thank you.

CARLIE: Now tell me the best thing about Jack—*Jake!* Don't you leap hurdles or rivers or chase speeding bullets or something?

JAKE: Hurdles. I'm on the track team.

CARLIE: How wonderful. Care to join us for a glass of champagne?

JAKE: Sure.

KARA: Jake. Would you mind…going—

CARLIE: Kara!

KARA: Going *ahead* to Twists. I just wanna finish dinner with Mom first.

CARLIE: He can stay. We have loads of food.

KARA: No. See, Dorien and Melody are already there. I think Melody was gonna try something crazy like smuggling a birthday cake into the club to surprise me.

CARLIE: Isn't that sweet.

KARA: If you go on, and tell them I'll be there later. I'm sure they're waiting for me.

JAKE: Sure.

KARA: That'd be great.

JAKE: I just wanted to come by. But…whatever the birthday girl wants.

KARA: I'll see you later.

JAKE: Nice to meet you, Mrs. Roberts.

CARLIE: If only briefly.

JAKE: Good night. *(To KARA.)* Later, OK? *(He gives her a quick kiss.)*

KARA: Promise.

(JAKE exits.)

CARLIE: Never in my life have I seen anyone behave so rudely.

KARA: He understands, Mom. Dinner tonight is just for us, remember?

CARLIE: Don't pull that on me, you little liar.

KARA: Liar?

CARLIE: You didn't want your precious boyfriend to be exposed to your Mother just because she's a little tipsy.

KARA: You're not tipsy, Mother. You're drunk.

CARLIE: How dare you! What business is it of yours?

KARA: What business? I can't bring anyone here. I can't have a party. I can't—

CARLIE: Do anything you want. I don't care.

KARA: Fine. I will!

CARLIE: Fine! Some thanks I get for trying to make a special evening for you. I worked all day in the kitchen, bought you a present—

KARA: And bought yourself two bottles of champagne.

CARLIE: I have only opened one of them.

KARA: But you've finished it. And you're gonna open the second one, and another and another. One is too many, and fifty's not enough for you.

CARLIE: Shut up!

(CARLIE hurls KARA's rose from JAKE onto the floor. KARA cries quietly.)

CARLIE: All right. You do what you like. I'm going out.

KARA: Mom—

CARLIE: I don't need to have my feelings hurt anymore. Nor do I need to spend my evening with an ungrateful daughter.

KARA: Please don't go. I'm sorry—

CARLIE: It's your fault! You don't want me here. I'll just go and you can invite the whole junior class into our home if you'd like.

KARA: I want to be with you.

CARLIE: Well you certainly don't act like it. Accusing me…You can spend your sweet sixteen by yourself. Dinner's in the oven. I don't want a bite of it. *(CARLIE leaves.)*

KARA: Mom…Please stay.

(CARLIE is gone.)

KARA: I need you. Mom.

(KARA stands alone. DAVID's voice brings her back to the present.)

DAVID: That's real honest, Kara.

KARA: So what.

(MUSIC in. KARA begins to dance. Her moves are strong, defiant.)

DAVID: So you're finding the truth. That's the only way a dance has power.

KARA: *(Dancing.)* It hurts.

DAVID: Keep going. Try to find the right steps.

(Her moves weaken. Then she shifts her direction, and begins a series of pivots and extensions that seem foreign to the dance so far.)

KARA: Melody. Why can't I be Melody?

DAVID: The right steps for *you.*

KARA: *(Dancing.)* In step…with Melody. She has power, she's pretty, everything.

(MELODY enters.)

KARA: My best friend. She has to be my best friend.

(KARA remembers seeing MELODY at school in the hallway, the day after her birthday. MUSIC out.)

MELODY: *(Calling back to a group of friends.)* Aleesha, tell Jamie I'll meet her at her locker, OK?

KARA: Hi.

MELODY: *(Offhand.)* Hi.

KARA: Thanks for the birthday card. Where'd you get it? It was funny—

MELODY: Don't mention it.

KARA: What's wrong?

MELODY: *Wrong?* How would you like it if you couldn't see your boyfriend for a month because your stupid best friend set you up?

KARA: I don't know what you're talking about.

MELODY: No? How come you told Jake that Dorien and I were going to Twists last night?

KARA: I didn't say you were going to be there for sure.

MELODY: Oh yeah? Well Jake calls my house and announces to my Mother that he'd looked all through Twists but Dorien and I weren't there. Did *she* know where we were? *Kara* said we were going to the club to celebrate her crappy birthday!

KARA: Melody—

MELODY: But you know where we were? At Dorien's house, 'cause his parents are out of town. I was having the most romantic night of my life, until Ber-ring, the phone rings and it's my *Mother!* Thanks a lot, friend.

KARA: I'm so sorry! Things were a little…crazy at my house last night. I needed an excuse—

MELODY: Yeah? If you're gonna lie, Kara, just screw yourself up, and leave me out of it.

(MUSIC in. MELODY exits.)

CARLIE: *(Appearing in one of the mirror-frames.)* Lies. Little liar.

KARA: *(To CARLIE.)* Don't accuse me.

CARLIE: Liar!

(KARA dances away from her mother, but she is confronted by MELODY.)

MELODY: *(Appearing in one of the mirror-frames.)* Just screw yourself up, Kara, and leave me out of it.

(KARA turns away from MELODY. She initiates a difficult series of moves. Her body twists and curves into unexpected shapes.)

DAVID: Every move affects the next move. It's like a chain. It's all linked.

KARA: *(Dancing.)* I didn't know he'd call, Melody. All I did was say—

DAVID: Every move you make connects to another move. Move your arm, it changes your back, move your foot—your balance changes. It's all connected.

KARA: *(Dancing.)* I'm sorry, Melody.

DAVID: Find the truth.

KARA: *(Dancing.)* I can't tell her the truth. I can't tell anyone.

CARLIE: *(A persistent memory in the mirror-frame.)* Little liar.

MELODY: *(Still in the mirror-frame.)* Just screw yourself up.

KARA: *(Dancing.)* Jake. Help me.

> *(JAKE enters. CARLIE and MELODY disappear.)*

KARA: Jake!

> *(KARA remembers meeting JAKE at the school's stadium bleachers later on the day after her birthday. MUSIC out.)*

JAKE: Close your eyes.

KARA: Why?

JAKE: Close 'em!

KARA: OK.

JAKE: Hold out your hands.

KARA: What're you doin'?

JAKE: Hold 'em out.

KARA: *(Giggling.)* I don't trust you.

> *(JAKE places a small box in KARA's hands.)*

JAKE: Happy birthday. I wanted to give you this last night. But things got kinda mixed up.

KARA: Yeah. Mom asked me to go to the movies with her after dinner. For my birthday. I couldn't say no. She was being so sweet. I'm really sorry.

JAKE: *(He whips the box back out of her hands.)* But you can't open it till you tell me the truth.

KARA: What?

JAKE: I saw you racin' outta the parking lot today. What was goin' on? Were you cryin' or something?

KARA: No! I was laughing. I'd been talking to Melody. And I was in a hurry cause I had to get to work.

> *(He gives her the box back.)*

JAKE: Why're you workin' at that pizza place anyway? Minimum wage. Who needs it!

KARA: I do. I've got to save $200, remember? For the dance program this summer.

JAKE: So I'll loan it to you.

KARA: You're crazy.

JAKE: That's right. Fast and crazy. About you. Say yes.

KARA: To what?

JAKE: To letting me loan you the money.

KARA: I couldn't do that, Jake. You don't have a job or anything.

JAKE: Doesn't matter. I got money.

KARA: You find it growing on trees, right?

JAKE: For you, I can do anything. Say yes.

KARA: I could probably pay you back by the end of the summer.

JAKE: It's no big deal. Say yes!

KARA: Yes. Yes, yes, yes! Good-bye pizza-land! Jake, you are the most wonderful, amazing—

JAKE: Fabulous human being. Now open it.

KARA: I couldn't take another thing from you.

JAKE: Open it!

KARA: *(Opening the box, she finds a very nice ring.)* Oh, Jake. This is gorgeous. But, I can't accept it.

JAKE: You don't wanna go together?

KARA: No. Yes!

JAKE: *(Laughing.)* Make up your mind!

KARA: It's just the ring. It must've cost a lot.

JAKE: Look in the bottom of the box.

KARA: Are you tryin' to make me faint or something? *(KARA pulls two tickets from the box.)* Tickets. To the dance?!

JAKE: I got it all set. We'll rent a limo with three other couples, all guys from the track team, so they're guaranteed to be cool. I'll get a tux. We'll go in style.

KARA: Jake, all this money—

JAKE: Lay off talkin' about money. It's not a problem. You've got to start trusting me, Kara.

KARA: I trust you like nobody else. You're the best—

JAKE: The best what?

KARA: The best thing that's ever happened to me.

JAKE: You wanna sail with me, Kara? *(He holds her.)* High above everything where nobody can touch us?

KARA: I'll go anywhere with you.

(MUSIC in. JAKE exits. KARA executes a series of dreamy moves, lost in the beauty of the memory of JAKE. She glides from one lovely step to the next.)

KARA: It's perfect again. I know the steps. I'll follow them anywhere.

DAVID: What happens next?

KARA: *(Sliding slowing across one of the dance bars into an almost prone position.)* Can't I stop here?

DAVID: You want the dance to end here?

KARA: I could stay here forever.

DAVID: You started with a bigger design. Don't you want all the parts to fit?

KARA: I've tried.

CARLIE: (Entering.) Kara.

KARA: (Jarred from her bliss, she dances away from CARLIE.) No! She'll ruin it. She ruins everything.

DAVID: This is the middle of the dance. The music can change.

KARA: It'll never change with her.

(KARA remembers a phone conversation with her mother. MUSIC out.)

CARLIE: Kara?

KARA: Mom, your partner from work called. She said you wanted to talk—

CARLIE: Yeah, I do.

KARA: Are you OK?

CARLIE: I'm fine—No. I'm not supposed to say that.

KARA: Mom, what *is* it?

CARLIE: I'm supposed to say, "I admit I am powerless over alcohol."

KARA: I'm coming over there.

CARLIE: No, honey.

KARA: Mom—

CARLIE: I'm not brave enough to see you yet today.

KARA: Can't you just tell me? What's going on?

CARLIE: I crashed last night, sweetheart. You must have seen me. Pretty picture I must have been sprawled on the floor.

KARA: I spent the night away last night—at Aleesha's. I left you a message. Oh God, I should've been there for you.

CARLIE: No, honey.

KARA: I should have been there!

CARLIE: Kara, stop it. I've got to take care of myself.

KARA: Is somebody with you?

CARLIE: I couldn't remember anything that happened last night. Nothing. It scared the hell out of me.

KARA: I'm so sorry.

CARLIE: It's what I needed, I guess.

KARA: I should have been there to help—

CARLIE: (Imitating herself.) "I don't need any help." Remember?

KARA: Yeah.

CARLIE: Well, I do. And I'm going to start by telling you how sorry I am. And how much I love you.

KARA: Oh I love you, too.

CARLIE: I know, honey.

KARA: I'll do anything—everything I can.

CARLIE: I'm getting help because of you.

(MUSIC in. KARA bursts into a joyous dance. Ebullient, she sweeps across the space with beautifully executed leaps and turns.)

KARA: *(Dancing.)* Because of me! All the times I've asked her to stop. I did it! New. It's all new now.

CARLIE: *(From her place for the phone conversation.)* I'm doing OK, Kara. It's one step at a time, but I'm doing OK.

KARA: *(Dancing.)* Light. Shooting from inside me. Beams of light. Cutting like a laser through everything.

DAVID: *That's* it. *That's* it!

CARLIE: I want to make things better for us, Kara. I will. I promise. I'll make up for a lot of lost time.

KARA: *(Dancing.)* I know what follows. I'm not afraid.

DAVID: Wait. The design. Something's missing.

KARA: *(Dancing.)* Melody. Melody! *(CARLIE exits.)*

(KARA remembers going to the shop where MELODY works. MUSIC out.)

MELODY: *(Entering.)* $4.21 is your change. You have a great day.

KARA: Excuse me, miss. Can I exchange this blouse?

(MELODY is silent.)

KARA: I've got a receipt.

MELODY: What do you want instead?

KARA: For you to stop being mad at me.

MELODY: Kara—

KARA: I'm sorry I got you in trouble. I never, ever wanted to.

MELODY: That's nice to know.

KARA: I *admit* I was stupid. There's been a lot of tension at my house. Jake kind of walked into the middle of it that night, and I had to get him out. *(MELODY listens, but she does not reply.)*

KARA: My Mom, she's been sick, but she's getting better. I want it to get better between us, too.

MELODY: It was just really bad timing.

KARA: I know. I'm sorry. But you get un-grounded before the dance, don't you?

MELODY: Barely.

KARA: How many ways can I say I'm *sorry!*

MELODY: Look, I don't know what's going on…with your Mom and all. But I really want to believe you.

KARA: You can. *(Playfully pleading.)* Please!!

MELODY: Oh, I'm a sucker for a sob story. *(The girls laugh.)*

KARA: So, you gonna let me exchange this?

MELODY: Why? You look good in blue.

KARA: Red'll look better in my resume shot.

MELODY *(Impressed.)* I see.

KARA: For the dance program application.

MELODY: And *who* is taking this picture of you?

KARA: I was hoping to ask a *friend* of mine.

MELODY: You'd *better* ask me. I don't want you gettin' bumped from that program cause some amateur took your picture.

KARA: Saturday afternoon. Your house. I'll bring the Jalapeño-cheddar Doritos.

MELODY: You're on. You get the film.

KARA: I'll get some for the dance, too. I want a thousand pictures of me and Jake Reynolds. I'm gonna plaster my walls with 'em.

MELODY: Bet you and Jake won't have half the fun that Dorien and I will.

KARA: What are you cookin' up?

MELODY: We got plans.

KARA: What? Tell me.

MELODY: *(Calling out to her boss.)* Clocking out for fifteen.

(The girls cross away from the sales counter to talk.)

MELODY: I told you that Dorien's uncle has this pontoon boat he keeps down on the river.

KARA: Yeah.

MELODY: Guess where Dorien and I are going to have a midnight picnic after the dance?

KARA: You're kidding. On a boat?

MELODY: We're not gonna ride anywhere. But he's gonna bring his stereo down. We're gonna listen to music.

KARA: That is the most romantic thing I've ever heard. So, uh, is this boat big enough for two more?

MELODY: This is a private party, girlfriend. No guests allowed.

KARA: *(Insinuatingly.)* I see!

MELODY: Kara! We're not gonna *do* anything. I just wanna be with him. He makes me feel so great, doesn't matter what we're doin'.

KARA: It's the same with Jake. God, does life get any better than this?

MELODY: Who cares. Right now, it's good. And right now is what counts.

KARA: Right now *and* Saturday afternoon.

MELODY: I'll make you look like a movie star!

KARA: God, I gotta go. Dance class.

MELODY: And me? I gotta sell fake designer clothes.

KARA: See you second period.

MELODY: Hey, Kara. Don't tell anybody about my prom night plans. I don't want it gettin' around. Some people at school, they'd get the wrong idea.

KARA: Promise.

MELODY: Glad you came by. *(She exits.)*

(KARA resumes her dance, springing happily across the space.)

KARA: Finally, it's all perfect! It all fits.

(KARA notices that there is no music. JAKE enters quickly.)

KARA: Jake.

(KARA remembers finding JAKE outside the school grounds, by some pay phones. He is distracted. He does not answer.)

KARA: Jake! Where've you been? I've been waiting for you in the library.

JAKE: I gotta stay out here.

KARA: By the pay phones? *(Joking.)* You expecting a call from one of your other girlfriends?

JAKE: I don't think that's funny.

KARA: I was just teasing. What's going on? You're doing a tiger imitation.

JAKE: I'm just…hanging out.

KARA: But you're all—

JAKE: *Lay off,* Kara.

KARA: *(Hurt, she is silent for a moment. But she cannot bare it.)* Wanna hear something great? I've got this great idea.

(JAKE ignores her.)

KARA: Don't you wanna hear it? My outrageously romantic idea for after the dance.

JAKE: Sure. Whatever.

KARA: Dorien's uncle has this boat, and he and Melody are going out on it after the dance. Cruisin' up and down the river. Isn't that a beautiful image—just two people and a boat.

JAKE: I don't have a boat. Sorry. OK?

KARA: Jake—

(The pay phone rings.)

KARA: That's weird. I'll answer it.

JAKE: *(Crossing in front of her.)* No.

(He picks up the receiver, listens quickly, then hangs it up again.)

KARA: What're you doing? You're acting really bizarre.

JAKE: Kara, listen. I've gotta go to class in a minute.

KARA: I know. And you still haven't kissed me.

JAKE: If the phone rings again, I want you to pick it up, then just hang it up again.

KARA: Why?

JAKE: Just *do* it. Please. *(He kisses her.)* You're great, Kara.

(JAKE exits.)

KARA: What's going on—

(The phone rings. KARA lets it ring a second time. She picks it up and listens for a moment, then speaks.)

KARA: Who is this? Who is this? Are you calling for Jake?

(The party on the other end hangs up. KARA stares at the phone.)

(MUSIC in.)

DAVID: What's wrong?

KARA: Nothing.

(KARA dances again. Her dance is now forced, tense. But the moves are easy, almost superficial.)

DAVID: Kara—

KARA: *(Stopping for an instant.)* He can't *do* this to me!

DAVID: Your dance.

(KARA begins again. Still forced, superficial.)

DAVID: It's losing its shape!

KARA: *(Dancing.)* I'll just go to class. Nothing is wrong. I'm fine.

DAVID: Don't do this.

KARA: Nothing is wrong. I am in control.

(KARA remembers a moment in the hallway at school. MUSIC grows.)

KARA: Hey Jamie, Aleesha! How's it goin'?

DAVID: That's fake. I don't believe you.

KARA: *(Talking to JAMIE and ALEESHA.)* Jake? Oh, he's great. We're great. Of course we're going to the dance. Then you know what we're gonna do? Yeah. Sail up and down the river.

DAVID: Kara—

KARA: *(Dancing again. Defiant.)* Nobody's life is as amazing as mine!

DAVID: What are you doing?

KARA: *(Dancing away from DAVID.)* Leave me alone.

(KARA remembers the next Saturday at MELODY's house. MUSIC out.)

MELODY: *(Entering.)* You ready?

KARA: Ready! Capture me on film! A lot of dancers try to look really solemn in their pictures. Maybe that's supposed to say you're extra-serious about what you do.

MELODY: I want to capture something else.

KARA: What? My sense of motion, of style—

MELODY: *(As she snaps a picture.)* I want a picture of the biggest mouth in town.

KARA: What?

MELODY: Of my "best friend" who doesn't even know how to *spell* trust.

KARA: What are you talking about?

MELODY: What were *you* talking about? Telling Aleesha and Jamie all about Dorien and me and the boat!

KARA: I didn't say anything—

MELODY: Funny they knew all about it! But they didn't quite get the story straight. According to them, it was *your* idea.

KARA: They're lying to you, Melody.

MELODY: *They* are lying to me?!

KARA: All I said was that you and Dorien and Jake and I—

MELODY: "You and Dorien and Jake and I" are doin' *nothing!* My plans were for Dorien and me alone. They were mine. My secret! What I do with my boyfriend is my business. I only told you because I thought I could trust you.

KARA: You *can*—

MELODY: Are you crazy? You blabbed it to Jake, too, didn't you? He came floatin' into fifth period and announced to the whole class that Dorien and me were sailin' to New Orleans Saturday night. What's with him, Kara? Something is way off with that guy.

KARA: There is nothing off about Jake.

MELODY: Open your eyes—

KARA: Look. I'm sorry you think I broke my promise. But you don't have to try to hurt me by saying things about Jake.

MELODY: You're messed up, Kara. You need some help.

KARA: I don't need any help. Leave me alone!

(MUSIC in. MELODY exits. CARLIE appears in one of the mirror-frames.)

CARLIE: I don't need any help.

KARA: Oh God.

DAVID: The pattern. I saw it in the beginning. It's repeating!

KARA: I'm not like her!

(Both CARLIE and MELODY enter from behind the frames. They crisscross the space around KARA, in harsh diagonal lines, surrounding her. KARA remains still, pleading, in the center.)

CARLIE: Little liar.

KARA: I'm sorry, Melody. Everything is crazy, slipping. Because of Jake. I needed his attention!

JAKE: *(Entering, joining the cacophony of memories, crossing harshly around KARA with the others.)* Lay off, Kara.

KARA: I'm so weak without him. I needed power. A secret is power. I used it. I *did* tell Jamie and Aleesha. I wanted to! It made me feel strong to have a secret—a secret I could *tell!*

(MUSIC becomes more and more intense. The "memories" close in on her.)

MELODY: You're messed up, Kara.

KARA: All my life, I could never tell anybody!

DAVID: The dance. It's not yours anymore.

KARA: Maybe Mom's getting better. But what about me!

DAVID: Your dance—

KARA: Why does everything have to fall apart! I hate it when it falls apart!

DAVID: *(Crossing to KARA.)* The music may be crazy, but the dance is yours.

JAKE: *(Stopping on KARA's other side, a complete change of tone.)* Sailing high above everything in a world of our own.

KARA: Take me there. Take me there!

DAVID: What are the steps?

KARA: I don't care. I don't care!

(All exit but JAKE. KARA remembers meeting JAKE right before KARA's dance class today. MUSIC out.)

KARA: Jake, you're late.

JAKE: Sorry.

KARA: I get worried when you don't do what you say you're going to.

JAKE: I said I'm sorry. Hey, I'll always be here for you, Kara. You know that.

KARA: God, I hope so. I need you. More than anything in the world.

JAKE: You mean that?

KARA: I don't know what I'd do without you.

JAKE: You love me?

KARA: I don't know what that means.

JAKE: Come on.

KARA: I must. I guess I must.

(They kiss.)

JAKE: Do something for me.

KARA: Anything.

JAKE: Call somebody for me.

KARA: Who?

JAKE: Just leave a message. Say I can't meet him today.

KARA: You can't meet *anybody* today. We're going to the post office together. To change your wonderful money into a wonderful check, so I can get my application in the mail and be *free* again.

JAKE: I need you to make the phone call first...from your house.

KARA: I don't have time to go home. I've got dance at 4:30. David kills me if I'm late.

JAKE: Then hurry. I'll meet you at the post office.

KARA: I wanted to go together.

JAKE: Kara, don't be so stupid. What does it matter?

KARA: I guess it doesn't.

JAKE: Here's the number.

(KARA takes a small piece of paper with the number from JAKE.)

KARA: Why can't you call this guy yourself?

JAKE: Tell him I'll meet him tomorrow. Same place.

KARA: Why won't you tell me what's going on?!

JAKE: Come on, honey. It's a secret.

KARA: I don't like secrets.

JAKE: I'm just...helpin' out a couple of guys. It's a business deal, OK?

KARA: What kind?

JAKE: *(Pacing.)* What, do I have to be cross-examined?

KARA: Why are you so nervous?

JAKE: I'm *not* nervous.

KARA: Are you high?

JAKE: I wish.

KARA: If something is wrong, let me help you. I can help.

JAKE: You got 500 bucks?

KARA: No.

JAKE: Then you can't help me.

KARA: Jake—

JAKE: Will you get outta here, for Christ's sake?! Just make the call. Make the call!

KARA: I don't understand.

JAKE: You wanna understand? OK. I've been helpin' out a couple of guys. Selling some stuff at school. And I messed up, OK?

KARA: You're dealing?!

JAKE: I'm *not* dealing. I'm just helpin' out.

KARA: Jake, why?

JAKE: Why? Why not! I mean, why the hell not? People are gonna do drugs,

Kara, so somebody's gotta sell 'em. And whoever sells 'em makes a lot of money, and that might as well be me.

KARA: That's crazy.

JAKE: What's crazy about wantin' to make some money? I'm not into slingin' pizzas for chump change.

KARA: Who are you getting it from? Who do you sell it to?

JAKE: I don't ask. I'm just a small link in a big chain. I don't care where the speed—

KARA: Speed!

JAKE: Or *any* of the stuff comes from, or who it trips out. I'm just on the business end.

KARA: Are you taking it too?

JAKE: You don't sample the goods, Kara. I'm not stupid.

KARA: Jake…You're better than this.

JAKE: Better than what?

KARA: You don't need this. You've got track—

JAKE: Runnin' around in circles for the rest of my life! No way. I need something bigger to get me outta this place. Now I got it.

KARA: What do you mean "out?" Where're you going? You can't leave me.

JAKE: I'm not goin' anywhere. But you're goin', right now to make one little phone call.

KARA: Can I please have the money you promised to loan me? I don't want to be a part of this.

JAKE: No phone call, no money.

KARA: What?

JAKE: *(Upset.)* I don't have any money to give you, OK?

KARA: You promised me!

JAKE: You make the call, and tomorrow I get the money, and you'll get your money, too.

(KARA is dumbfounded. Desperate.)

JAKE: Look, I wouldn't be doin' this if somebody didn't need to borrow $200.

KARA: Don't blame me. You can't blame *me*.

JAKE: You got me into this. Now you've got to get me out.

KARA: No! *(KARA reaches for JAKE. He pulls away.)*

JAKE: Help me, Kara. Please. *(JAKE exits.)*

(MUSIC in. KARA turns away from JAKE frantically. She is half pacing, spinning, stumbling.)

DAVID: A pattern. Repeating. Break out!

KARA: I can't help him. I can't always be *helping* somebody. I don't need him. Mom. She has some money. I'll get it from her.

(KARA remembers racing to her house after arguing with JAKE. MUSIC out.)

KARA: Mom, I need to talk to you. Mom. *(KARA sees her Mother. CARLIE is drunk.)* Mom!

CARLIE: Welcome home, princess.

KARA: Oh my God.

CARLIE: How was school? Learn anything?

KARA: Why do you always do this to me. You are *worthless* to me!

CARLIE: I just slipped off the ole cart, no, wagon, isn't that what they say—

KARA: Where's your wallet. I need some money.

CARLIE: Afraid the cupboard is bare, princess.

KARA: God, have you drunk up your last dime? Great. OK. I've got seventy-five dollars. *(KARA searches for it.)* I'll call the dance people. Tell them I'll get the rest somehow. Where *is* it?

CARLIE: Afraid the cupboard is bare.

KARA: My money. Mom. Where is it?

CARLIE: I had a few bills to pay. A few drinks to pay—

KARA: *No!!*

(MUSIC in. KARA struggles to dance again, but the memory of JAKE stops her.)

JAKE: *(Entering, crossing to KARA.)* Just a small link in a big chain. Make the call. What does it matter? Who does it hurt?

DAVID: Your dance.

KARA: *(KARA struggles to regain control. She dances across the space, away from JAKE, in a series of extensions and contractions.)* I'm going to this dance program. I'm going to be accepted and I'm gonna go. *None* of you can stop me from getting what I want.

JAKE: Have you ever really gotten what you want?

(The question stops KARA. She freezes with her arms open, outstretched.)

JAKE: From anybody?

KARA: No.

CARLIE: *(Crossing toward KARA from behind a mirror-frame.)* I don't need you mumbling around me. I don't need you at all.

KARA: *(Breaking out of her needy pose, dancing away from CARLIE.)* I don't need *you!*

JAKE: Just a small link in a big chain. Who cares? Get what you want.

KARA: *(Dancing.)* I want to dance.

(CARLIE and JAKE remain. They are obstacles—both physically and emotionally—as KARA struggles to dance.)

DAVID: You're setting the moves.

CARLIE: I love to see you dance.

KARA: *(Dancing.)* Then why can't you see me. I want you to see me and not a bottle!

JAKE: Just make the call. Then we'll get the money. And you'll get what you want.

MELODY: *(Entering from behind one of the mirror-frames.)* Don't tell anybody, Kara. It's just between us.

KARA: Secrets. Secrets are OK. The call…it could be a secret!

CARLIE: It's our secret.

JAKE: Nobody'll know. What does it matter?

MELODY: *(Overlapping.)* It doesn't matter.

CARLIE: *(Overlapping.)* It doesn't matter.

ALL THREE: It doesn't matter.

(All freeze. MUSIC stops. KARA is isolated—driven into a corner by her thoughts. DAVID steps forward.)

DAVID: The music's playing. But it's your dance. How do you want it to end?

KARA: Just a small link. What does it matter? What could happen? If I make the call…What if I just make the call.

(MUSIC in. A different music, perhaps merely an electronic pulse. All characters exit, as KARA imagines the future consequences of making the call. She imagines picking up the phone.)

KARA: Hello. I'm calling for Jake. He can't meet you today. He'll meet you tomorrow. Good-bye. *(She hangs up.)* I did it, Jake. I did it.

(Sound of POLICE SIRENS. JAKE runs on. They are both trapped in a barricade created by the dance bars.)

KARA: You promised nothing would happen!

JAKE: *(As if responding to a policeman.)* Jake Reynolds. Seventeen.

KARA: Don't tell them anything. Tell them you made a mistake. Tell them—

JAKE: 634 Edgefield Road.

KARA: Tell them you won't do it again. Ever—

(KARA and JAKE shift positions. KARA is now responding to a policeman.)

KARA: Kara. Kara Roberts. Sixteen. I didn't do anything!

(The SIREN gets louder and louder.)

KARA: *No!*

(KARA breaks away. JAKE exits. MUSIC out. Her fantasy stops.)

KARA: This way. What if…I made the call this way. *(She fantasizes again.*

MUSIC in. She imagines picking up the phone.) Hello? Please. Leave my boyfriend alone. He doesn't need you, or your drugs. Get out of our lives. Leave us alone.

(KARA hangs up. JAKE enters. He is relaxed.)

KARA: I did it, Jake. Now you're out of it. See? It's easy.

JAKE: Easy.

KARA: You'll never be scared again. I'll never be scared.

JAKE: That's 'cause we're in now, Kara.

KARA: No. See, I told them to leave us alone. Now they will. We're out. Please say we're out—

JAKE: We've gotta trust 'em.

KARA: No—

JAKE: Sail with me, Kara.

KARA: With you—

JAKE: *(Offering her a joint.)* You'll go anywhere with me, won't you?

KARA: *(Sinking into his arms, slowly reaching for the joint.)* Yes.

JAKE: And you'll help me make just one more call—

KARA: No!

(KARA breaks out and stops the fantasy. JAKE exits. MUSIC stops.)

KARA: This way. I want it to end this way.

(MUSIC in. She grabs the phone.)

KARA: Hello. Jake can't meet you today. But he'll meet you tomorrow. Just bring us the money. And we'll never have to think about this again. It will all be over, and I'll go to the summer dance program, and Jake will be fine, and Mom will be fine. All right!!

(She hangs up. MUSIC out. SILENCE. Kara turns frantically, waiting for the next imagined disaster. Nothing. But then her memories and fantasies mingle. MUSIC in.)

KARA: I did it Jake.

JAKE: *(Entering.)* You said you'd do anything for me. And you did.

KARA: Promise you'll never do it again. No more drugs. Anything. Please. Promise.

JAKE: I promise.

CARLIE: *(Overlapping JAKE's "I promise.")* I promise, Kara, I'll never touch a drop again.

(CARLIE and JAKE converge on KARA, one on each side. KARA shrinks.)

JAKE: I'll never hurt you.

CARLIE: I never want to hurt you, honey.

KARA: Promise?

JAKE: *(Roughly.)* Just *do* it!

CARLIE: *(Roughly.)* Do whatever you want.

KARA: Please—

MELODY: *(Running on, taking KARA's hands, they spin together in a circle, little-girl-like.)* It'll be our secret, Kara. Promise.

KARA: I'll keep all your secrets, Melody. That's what a friend is, right?

MELODY: *(Releasing KARA's hands sharply, abandoning her.)* Just screw yourself up with your lies.

KARA: *(To MELODY.)* No. I need you—

CARLIE: *(Holding open arms out to KARA.)* Come here, princess.

KARA: *(Running into her mother's arms.)* I promise. I'll never tell anybody. I won't ever let anybody know.

MELODY: You lied to me.

CARLIE: Trust me, princess.

(KARA wrenches out of her Mother's arms, and draws away from all the "voices.")

JAKE: You can trust me.

MELODY: I trusted you.

KARA: Trust?! I don't know how to trust! Why should I know how?

JAKE: What does it matter? Who does it hurt?!

KARA: It hurt me! It *hurts* me! And I've hurt you. Hurt you…

(MUSIC out. KARA is near collapse, fighting back tears.)

DAVID: Kara…You've *got* to talk to me.

(KARA shakes her head, and tries to compose herself.)

DAVID: Did something happen before you came in here today?

(KARA still doesn't answer.)

DAVID: I've never seen you like this.

KARA: I have to dance. Don't make me stop.

DAVID: Then dance. Dance till you drop!

(KARA begins a powerful move, but she cannot complete it. Finally, at long last, she crumbles.)

DAVID: Kara—

KARA: I want…my dance to be beautiful and honest. And I don't know how. I'm stuck in something bigger than me—a pattern. My Mom…my boyfriend…*me!* I want out!

DAVID: What?

KARA: I'm alone. Help me get out. I can't do it alone. Help me.

DAVID: Out of what?

KARA: It's like a web…all tangled…we keep hurting each other. I've got to stop hurting—

DAVID: Kara—

KARA: Help me!

DAVID: I…look, we'll get you somewhere…talk to somebody. A counselor, something.

KARA: Please.

DAVID: We'll get you out, Kara. Alright?

(KARA nods. DAVID helps her to her feet.)

DAVID: I didn't know.

KARA: I didn't tell. (KARA smiles sadly.) Secrets.

(DAVID puts his arm around her. She slowly puts her arm around DAVID. They exit the studio together.)

END OF PLAY

Broken Rainbows

ORIGINAL PRODUCTION

Broken Rainbows was commissioned by and first presented at the Round House Theatre, Silver Spring, Maryland (Artistic Director, Jerry Whiddon) on September 5, 1991. It was directed by Sue Ott Rowlands; the set design was by Elizabeth Jenkins; the costume design was by Rosemary Pardee; the sound design was by Neil McFadden. The stage manager was David Dossey. The cast was as follows:

GINA INGRIM . . . . Toyin Fadope

DAMOND INGRIM. . . . . Godfrey L. Simmons, Jr.

JOEL COHEN . . . . Jason Kravits

ELLY COHEN. . . . . Kate Bryer

Broken Rainbows toured to junior highs and high schools throughout the Washington, D.C. metropolitan area for three seasons. The performance was often followed by a discussion, moderated by the stage manager, with the actors, who remained in role.

CAST OF CHARACTERS

GINA INGRIM: Seventeen years old, African-American, an aspiring singer/songwriter

DAMOND INGRIM: Nineteen years old, Gina's brother

JOEL COHEN: Eighteen years old, Italian-Jewish-American Gina's classmate

ELLY COHEN: Thirty-eight years old, Italian-Jewish-American, Joel's mother

Several voice-overs and radio announcers

SETTING

A middle-income neighborhood in Montgomery County, Maryland (or any suburban area near a large city)

TIME

The first few weeks of a hot Washington summer

SCENE ONE

The playing space is divided into two areas. One represents the Ingrims' apartment, the other the Cohens'. Despite the division, the playing space, especially the center, must remain flexible and open to allow for fluid movement in and out of multiple locations. Only minimal props should be used.

Taped piano music, the accompaniment for GINA's song, is playing. Seventeen-year-old GINA INGRIM enters. She turns up the tape in her tune-box. Her brother, nineteen-year-old DAMOND, enters. He has his saxophone.

GINA: *(Singing.)* "Do you think? Could it be?
    Is there a place that shines like in my dreams?"
DAMOND: Sing it, Gina.
GINA: *(Singing.)* "A place where we could go
    No one would have to know
    A place on the other side of now."
DAMOND: Work it! Work it!
GINA: *(Singing.)* "Where we could dance. We could run
    As fast as light, sail right up to the sun."
    (DAMOND joins in, providing additional accompaniment with his sax. During this verse, first eighteen-year-old JOEL COHEN enters, then his mother, ELLY, into the space that will represent their apartment. They remain still and separate from each other throughout the song.)
GINA: *(Singing.)* "And leave our fear behind
    Take courage and we'll find
    The place on the other side of now.
    Ride over the rainbow till it ends
    Touch a star and wish for what might be.
    Catch the wind and hold it in your heart and fly
    To a world that starts with you and me.
    To the place on the other side of now.
    The place on the other side of now."
    (A tableau of the four characters, with GINA at the center, as the song concludes. DAMOND and GINA begin their scene. ELLY and JOEL shift positions, making it clear that they are not a part of the same scene.)
DAMOND: Watch out! Gina Ingrim is hot!
GINA: Rocketin' to the top!
DAMOND: Gotta bop!

(DAMOND bursts into a jazzy beebop tune on his sax.)
GINA: Damond, let's do it again.
(DAMOND keeps playing.)
GINA: Damond! With my tape.
DAMOND: You really write that song?
GINA: It's my "Over the Rainbow." Like Dorothy's in *The Wizard of Oz.*
DAMOND: I can see you now in munchkin land. Hopping around with all
those little white people. *(Singing in a silly, high voice.)* "We're off to see
the Wizard—"
GINA: It's *my* version!
DAMOND: *(Singing.)* "The Wonderful Wizard of Oz."
GINA: There's a black *Wizard of Oz*, too. *The Wiz.* Michael Jackson played
the scarecrow in the movie.
DAMOND: *(Singing Michael Jackson style.)* "Awowwh, if I only had a brain.
Dangerous!"
GINA: *(Turning on the tape.)* Let's take it again. From the top.
DAMOND: That you playing?
GINA: I can't play this good. A guy at school made it for me. He's got every
song—
DAMOND: Thought *you* got all the songs. *(Teasing, imitating her.)* "*Every*
song, *inside* me."
GINA: I *said* I got music…a singer within. I'm just openin' the doors and
lettin' her out.
DAMOND: Well, keep lightin' the way, little sister. I gotta go earn my daily
bread.
*(Music fades as JOEL now begins a scene with his mother, ELLY. The two
scenes continue simultaneously.)*
JOEL: I gotta get to work, Mom.
ELLY: Joel—
GINA: Damond, you late again?
JOEL: I'll miss the bus.
DAMOND: "Late" is no longer in my vocabulary.
*(DAMOND gets ready to go and GINA puts on her headphones as the scene
continues.)*
ELLY: Never did we used to take the bus.
JOEL: It's no hassle.
ELLY: Two cars we had and you had nice clothes.
JOEL: What's wrong with my clothes?
ELLY: I *hate* that I did this to you.

JOEL: Mom, it's too early for tragedy.

ELLY: I won't say another word.

(Pause as JOEL picks up his backpack, pulling together what he needs for the day.)

ELLY: Your Father did this to you.

JOEL: You gonna study for your test today?

ELLY: Twenty-one years, twenty-one and a half, then boom! Divorce. No discussion. Finito.

JOEL: I'm going out on the trucks today. First time.

ELLY: "Who is she," I say to him. Leaves me counting pennies over an empty Crock-Pot. Ah, scusi, in our lovely new apartment, we don't have a Crock-Pot, or a dishwasher—

JOEL: We got a microwave.

ELLY: And a triple lock on the door. What a neighborhood.

JOEL: We'll get used to it.

ELLY: Have you seen a single person around here like us? Well?

JOEL: What's "like us," Mom?

GINA: Damond, remember to stop by Hecht's layaway and pick up Momma's new rug.

DAMOND: That information is stored in the computer of my mind.

GINA: *(Teasing.)* Your microchip has crashed more than once, cyber-head.

DAMOND: I got new software, baby. Called "jumpin' to the front of the movie line."

GINA: What?

JOEL: I'll see ya, Mom.

DAMOND: Later, sister.

ELLY: Work hard, but don't get overheated.

JOEL: I'll speak to the weatherman.

GINA: Stay cool, trash man.

ELLY: Always say good morning to your boss. *(Calling after him.)* And don't forget! Get the application for that internship!

JOEL and DAMOND: OK!

(The two boys exit from their apartments at the same time. They see one another, but neither boy greets the other. They cross to the bus.)

SCENE TWO

Upbeat rock music underscores the entire scene. At center stage JOEL and DAMOND are on a crowded bus on the way to work. JOEL is reading a magazine. DAMOND is listening and occasionally rocking-out to his Walkman. As the scene progresses, they mime the bus stopping, other passengers getting on and off, the subtle competition for empty seats.

Simultaneously, GINA is in her apartment, talking on the phone. ELLY is in her apartment, writing a letter. The focus moves back and forth, and is punctuated by action in the bus mime sequence.

GINA: I'll get *one* of 'em, Momma. They're hiring next week. Shoot, I could run a record store all by myself. *(Pause.)* Uh-huh, I got my business teacher to write one for me. Mrs. Emilyo. *(Pronouncing it again for her Mother's sake.)* E-mil-yo. *(Pause.)* Momma, if you can work two jobs, I can work one.

ELLY: "Dear Ray, ex-husband, Shmuck of the planet."
(She rips up her letter and starts again.)

GINA: I'll keep up. This job will *help* me with my music.
(Momma is giving her "Follow your dreams" speech. GINA's lines are in response to it.)

GINA: I know. Don't worry. I *am* dreamin', Momma! You'd be all over me if I wasn't.

ELLY: "You may have heard that I lost my job. You may also have heard that we lost the house."

GINA: We're fine. I'm *proud* of you. We're catchin' up, Momma.

ELLY: "You may also have heard that your son is now a garbage collector."

GINA: Not "trash," Momma. Damond's working in the recycling industry. He recycles...*(Not knowing what else to call it.)* Trash.

ELLY: "Ray, I don't want to ask you this, but we won't make it through the next couple of months. I'm trying to change careers, and Momma's in this new nursing home—"

GINA: I think Damond's tryin' this time.

ELLY: "For Joel's sake, send some money. *(Genuinely.)* Please."

GINA: I love you, too.

ELLY: *(Looking up, saying what she wishes she could write.)* I never, ever wanted it to end like this, Ray. I miss you. Miss *us. (Then, writing quickly.)* "Sincerely, Elly."

(The bus comes to a halt. DAMOND steps out in front of the hesitating JOEL. Music swells and ELLY throws down her pen. ELLY and GINA exit as the next scene begins.)

SCENE THREE

JOEL and DAMOND are at the recycling center. DAMOND is hanging out, joking with the [unseen] others. JOEL says "hi" to a couple of people, but soon sits quietly.

VOICE-OVER: OK, everybody. Listen up. Training finished last Friday. Let's congratulate again our outstanding trainee from the first week, Joel Cohen. *(DAMOND claps unenthusiastically.)*

VOICE-OVER: Today, you hit the streets. Two collectors go with each caravan.

DAMOND: *(Raising his hand.)* I'll distribute the assignments.

VOICE-OVER: We've posted them on the board, but thanks, Damond.

DAMOND: No problem.

JOEL: *(Raising his hand.)* I assume we report back at 4:45.

DAMOND: *(Under his breath.)* 4:50.

VOICE-OVER: Clock back in at 4:50. Good luck, everybody. Let's go.
(JOEL and DAMOND both cross to a large posted list, mimed downstage, to look for their assignments.)

JOEL: Cohen…

DAMOND: Ingrim…"Peli-can tram." *(Calling out.)* OK. Who's consumin' aluminum with the man here?

JOEL: I am.

DAMOND: You sure you're not lost little guy?

JOEL: What's that supposed to mean? I'm not the only—

DAMOND: Hold up. I mean lost from Munchkin-land!

JOEL: *(Sarcastically enthusiastic.)* Hey, that's original. Usually it's "short-stuff" or "shrimp." But Munchkin, that's good. Real good.

VOICE-OVER: Let's go, boys.

DAMOND: *(To JOEL.)* Come on, hotshot. We're off to see the Wizard.
(DAMOND crosses off, laughing. JOEL pauses, then follows.)

SCENE FOUR

ELLY and GINA cross into their apartments. ELLY is holding a book, studying, as she paces around the apartment, and crosses to her stove to stir a very strong smelling soup. GINA is listening to her tape, very loudly, as she sings along, experimenting with vocal flourishes for the song.

GINA: *(Singing.)* "Ride over the rainbow till it ends, touch a star…"
    (GINA continues the song under ELLY's lines.)
ELLY: "On a thirty-year fixed rate mortgage, at eight and a quarter, with two and seven-eighths points, each point paid is roughly the equivalent of one-eighth of a percentage of the oregano—*(She can't find it.)* What? No oregano, how can I cook! *(Referring to the music.)* How can I study.
GINA: *(Singing.)* "Do you think—"
ELLY: I can't think.
GINA: *(Singing.)* "Could it be." *(Stopping.)* A nasty smell! What's she cookin' over there?!
ELLY: *(Trying to cover her ears and cook and read loudly to herself.)* "Interest rates on a seven-twenty-three are constant for that period, then generally are adjusted to a new rate—"
GINA: *(Trying to sing with her nose plugged.)* "A place on the other side of—"
ELLY: That's it.
GINA: What *is* that!
    (The two women burst out of their apartment doors and into the hallway at the exact same moment. Both are a bit startled.)
GINA: Is something burning?
ELLY: Pardon?
GINA: The smell. I thought something was burning.
ELLY: No, it's cacciucoo.
GINA: What?
ELLY: Cacciu—call it soup. Are you the one with the music?
GINA: Yeah.
ELLY: Could you turn it down.
GINA: Yeah.
ELLY: Thanks.
    (She starts to go back in.)
GINA: Your apartment was empty for so long. I forgot about the noise.
ELLY: It's not empty now. *(Awkward pause.)* You can smell what I'm cooking?
GINA: Our kitchens have a common wall. We share a vent.

ELLY: I'll watch the smells.
(She starts to go back in, then stops.)
GINA: It's cool, now that I know what it is.
ELLY: Don't think I don't like music. My son plays piano.
GINA: Really?
ELLY: I'm just trying to concentrate over here.
GINA: I've got headphones.
ELLY: Good. Thank you.
(ELLY crosses quickly back into her apartment. GINA goes back into hers.)

SCENE FIVE

JOEL and DAMOND enter with large crates. They mime picking up smaller crates and dumping cans, bottles, and newspapers into their crates, then into the large bins on the truck.

DAMOND: Man, this must be a six-pack-a-day neighborhood. What're they doin' with all these nasty cans?
JOEL: People don't think about it. Buy a Coke, drink it, throw the can away, like that's the end of it.
DAMOND: "The end" is me busting my butt.
JOEL: "The end" is environmental catastrophe!
DAMOND: Whatever you say, Professor Greenpeace. *(Muttering.)* Why'd they have to paint these trucks all circus-lookin'? Bright colors and kiddie names—"Paper tiger" for white paper, "Mr. News" for newspaper—
JOEL: The trucks are supposed to attract attention, so people will think about recycling.
(Sound of the horn of a car driving past. DAMOND ducks behind one of the bins.)
DAMOND: Outta my way, man.
JOEL: What're you doin'?
DAMOND: Damn!
JOEL: What's the deal?
DAMOND: That was Lamont!
JOEL: Huh?
DAMOND: Lamont, man!
JOEL: Don't want your friends seein' ya doin' this?
DAMOND: Damn straight.

JOEL: Why're you working this job, if you don't care about the environment?

DAMOND: I care about the environment of my wallet. My paycheck.

JOEL: Trash for cash, huh?

DAMOND: Just puttin' in my time on the bottom, so I can step up to the top. *(Pause.)*

JOEL: Listen, I don't know too many people around here, so I'll stay on the front line.

DAMOND: Yeah?

JOEL: Feel free to hide behind me.

DAMOND: *(Laughing.)* The new kid in town, huh?

JOEL: Very observant.

DAMOND: And you haven't had my tour of the neighborhood?

JOEL: Huh?

DAMOND: Step right up, Munchkin-man. Damond's Grayline cruise of our fair community is pullin' out.

(They have finished this collection sight. They jump on the truck. They mime the truck pulling out and moving down the street. The truck's radio is on.)

RADIO: Hot summer in the Capital City! Stay out of the sun, get into some fun!

(Rock/rap music begins, and underscores the tour.)

DAMOND: On your left we have three to five small streets, with thirty to fifty identical houses, filled with three to five hundred identical people.

JOEL: What're you talking about?

DAMOND: Asians, man. Every one of 'em. From China, Vietnam, I don't know where else. Millions of 'em. Count 'em!

JOEL: Right.

DAMOND: Down *that* road you will find enchilada land.

JOEL: Hispanics live over there?

DAMOND: "His"panics, "her"spanics—

JOEL: You're crazy.

DAMOND: Then further over, *way* over, locked away on your right, we find the land of milk and honey. God's *chosen*—

JOEL: Yeah, OK.

DAMOND: The Goldbergs, the Silverbergs, the Moneybergs—

JOEL: I'm Jewish, OK? Lay off.

(The truck comes to a stop. MUSIC fades as the boys get off to do another collection.)

DAMOND: Sorry, man.

JOEL: Half-Jewish. Maybe three-quarters.

DAMOND: You don't know?

JOEL: My Dad was—is—Jewish, and my Mom is Italian-Jewish, but she—

DAMOND: All Italians are Catholics, man. Mafia—

JOEL: Not all…Forget it. It's not worth it.

DAMOND: Whatever you say, man.

(They work in silence for a moment.)

DAMOND: I'll chill on the Jewish jokes. Catholic, too.

JOEL: You're too kind.

DAMOND: But d'you hear the one about the Spik and his girlfriend—

(The sound of the truck horn.)

JOEL: Hustle, man. *(Looking back.)* Come on, hustle.

(JOEL bustles off, but DAMOND takes his time with his bin. Both exit.)

SCENE SIX

Late afternoon, a few days later. GINA is in her apartment. She is talking to herself as she enters.

GINA: "Yasmeen Asi Ingrim." No. "Faida Yasmeen Kahlil Ingrim." Too long. "Accepting her Grammy for the best new vocalist of the year, Gina Yasmeen Kahlil Ingrim!!"

(DAMOND enters bouncing a basketball on the court outside.)

DAMOND: Gina. Yo! Gina!

GINA: *(Calling back.)* I'm workin' on my name.

DAMOND: You better work on your game. You owe me.

GINA: Tomorrow.

DAMOND: You want a saxophone player next time you sing?

GINA: Today.

DAMOND: Now, superstar!

(GINA crosses out quickly. As DAMOND does a few fancy moves on the court, ELLY crosses through en route to her apartment. DAMOND, unintentionally, almost runs her down. ELLY shrinks back from him.)

DAMOND: Sorry. I wasn't looking.

(ELLY does not respond.)

DAMOND: I said, "Sorry."

(ELLY crosses rapidly to her apartment. DAMOND looks after her, then does a playful threatening gesture, making fun of her fear.)

DAMOND: *(To himself.)* I was just trying to mug, assault, and sell you crack. *(Disgusted.)* Shiii—

JOEL: *(Entering.)* What's up, Damond.

DAMOND: *(Passing the ball to JOEL.)* Think fast, hotshot.

JOEL: Thanks for the invitation. But no thanks.

DAMOND: Don't like basketball?

JOEL: *(Referring to his height.)* What do you think?

(JOEL flips the ball back to DAMOND and is turning to leave as GINA enters.)

GINA: OK, Damond. *One* game. That's—*(She sees Joel and recognizes him.)* Hi.

JOEL: Hi.

GINA: How ya doin'? I thought I saw you a couple of days ago. But you don't—

JOEL: Yeah. I do. I live in 306.

GINA: Damond, this is Joel…I can't remember your last name.

DAMOND and JOEL: Cohen.

GINA: You guys know each other? Damond, Joel made the tape of my song for me. "The Other Side of Now." This is great! You live next door? I must have met your Mother.

JOEL: I've gotta see if she's home.

DAMOND: She's home.

GINA: The tape's really helped me.

JOEL: You're welcome.

GINA: Thank you.

JOEL: It was for a project at school. No big deal. I'll see ya.

(He exits quickly.)

GINA: Bye.

DAMOND: Why don't ya try to find guys your own size, tall woman?

GINA: I barely know him. But man, he is *good* on piano.

DAMOND: Wish he was *good* at the recycle-circus.

GINA: He works with you?

DAMOND: Our "team's" been dead last every day this week. He ain't exactly Hercules.

GINA: Poor guy.

DAMOND: I'm the one takin' up the slack. *(Tossing her the ball.)* Come on. One-on-one.

(GINA and DAMOND begin a game as ELLY enters her apartment.)

GINA: Take it easy. It's too hot to play rough.

DAMOND: I am hot all the time.

GINA: *(Holding the ball.)* Wonder why he never came over—

DAMOND: Gina—

GINA: Just knocked on the door or something?

DAMOND: Foul on Number *Zero!* For runnin' off at the mouth.

> *(GINA laughs and starts the ball moving. GINA and DAMOND play throughout the top of the following scene. JOEL joins ELLY in their apartment. ELLY is distracted.)*

ELLY: I burned your supper.

JOEL: *(His preferred cheery greeting.)* "Welcome home, son."

ELLY: Welcome home, son, and I still burned your supper. I left it in the oven when I went out—

JOEL: I'll go get us something.

ELLY: I put it on low, it cooks high. Just get yourself something. I won't eat.

JOEL: Mom—

ELLY: I'm on a diet.

JOEL: No you're not. *(Intercepting her as she bustles past.)* Mom. Sit. Sit!

> *(ELLY sits quietly. DAMOND and GINA exit the basketball court. JOEL sits to begin a conversation with his Mother, but at first they are silent.)*

JOEL: So. Did you study all day?

ELLY: No.

JOEL: Ma—

ELLY: My brains were numbed by the noise from the street and the balls bouncing against the building—

JOEL: How much longer before the big test?

ELLY: I don't know.

JOEL: How can you not know?

ELLY: *(Getting up.)* I don't know.

JOEL: Ma—

ELLY: I lost the letter that tells me when it is.

JOEL: So call 'em up.

ELLY: I want to read it from the letter. All right?

JOEL: What does it matter?

ELLY: It matters. *(ELLY stops, trying to keep herself from bursting into tears.)* All right?

> *(JOEL is very uncomfortable, awkward, confused by her mood.)*

JOEL: I'll help you look for it.

ELLY: Don't.

JOEL: Is it in your purse?

ELLY: I don't need a mother, Joel. I am the mother, here! *I'm* the mother.

(Tense, awkward pause.)

JOEL: There's a Chinese place on the corner. My treat.

ELLY: I don't want you walking around here at night.

JOEL: It's not night.

(He starts to exit.)

ELLY: Joel—

JOEL: I'll be back in a minute.

ELLY: *(Saying what she really needs to say.)* Your father called today.

(JOEL stops, but is silent.)

ELLY: He said…he's getting married. He wanted you to know. So…now you know.

(They stand in painful silence. Neither knows how to reach out to the other one.)

JOEL: That all?

ELLY: Yeah.

(JOEL exits his apartment. At the same moment, GINA is exiting hers. She is drinking a soda.)

GINA: *(Calling back to her apartment.)* I'm just gonna sit on the steps. It's too hot up here. *(Sees JOEL.)* Hey. What're you doin' hurryin' on a night like this?

(JOEL stops.)

GINA: All I wanna do is cool down.

JOEL: *(Feeling the irony.)* Me too.

GINA: There's a breeze here if you wanna sit.

(JOEL pauses, but then crosses to the steps and sits.)

GINA: We got so many fans goin' sounds like a church choir, all hummin' at different pitches. You gotta air conditioner?

JOEL: No.

GINA: We're supposed to get one next week. My Momma, she's crazy. Bought a rug before she bought an air conditioner, in summer! But she had her heart set on this braided rug, and Mommas deserve to get what they want sometimes.

JOEL: Sometimes they can't get it.

(Pause.)

GINA: How's the job? You like it?

JOEL: Gets pretty old pretty fast.

GINA: But it's important.

JOEL: You don't have to tell me. My nickname at my old school was the enviro-maniac!

GINA: *(Laughing.)* What?

JOEL: I used to take ice tea for lunch in a thermos every day so I didn't add another bottle to the pile. I tried to organize people in my old neighborhood to subscribe to the *Post* in pairs! I get pretty crazy about it. I wanna make a difference, y'know?

GINA: My Momma says if you wanna change the way things are, start with yourself. Then it'll ripple out. Change other people.

JOEL: I'm gonna get—*(Correcting himself.)* I'm *applying* for this other job— a management internship the company's offering. If I could get that, it'd be so great. It's more money, too, which would also be pretty great.

GINA: You'd be a recycling manager?

JOEL: Training to be one, yeah.

GINA: Work for it. You'll get it.

JOEL: I really want it.

GINA: Then you'll get it. So I shouldn't toss this bottle in any ol' dumpster around you, huh?

(They share a laugh.)

GINA: If *I* were cleaning up the planet, I'd do a lot more than pick up the garbage. I'd turn the world into the land of Oz—an Emerald City.

JOEL: *(Laughs.)* Over the rainbow, right?

GINA: You think it's that far?

(JOEL looks at her.)

JOEL: That song I recorded for you, it was some kinda Oz-song, wasn't it?

GINA: Yeah. Didn't you keep a copy?

JOEL: No. Sorry.

GINA: I'll write the words out for you. Maybe we can play it…"du-et" it—

ELLY: *(From offstage.)* Joel!

JOEL: Yeah.

ELLY: *(Entering.)* That *is* your voice—*(She sees GINA.)* Oh.

GINA: Hi.

JOEL: Mom, this is Gina—

ELLY: We've met.

GINA: I didn't know till the other day we had Joel in common.

JOEL: We know each other from school.

ELLY: Good. That's good. Are you going to get some dinner, Joel?

JOEL: I'm on my way—

GINA: I didn't mean to keep you—

ELLY: I didn't mean to interrupt. I can go—

JOEL: Ma, no. I'm going. 'Night, Gina.

GINA: See ya.
(ELLY watches JOEL exit.)
GINA: *(To ELLY.)* Good night.
ELLY: 'Night.
(ELLY and GINA exit.)

SCENE SEVEN

Two weeks later. Music underscores the entire scene. More driving, hard beat. Hotter. JOEL and DAMOND are back on the bus. It is crowded, hot. GINA crosses on to the front steps of the apartment house. She is painting her nails.

DAMOND: *(Pulling off his Walkman headphones.)* Yo, Joel. Mastermind! Don't we change trucks today? Been two weeks.
JOEL: Maybe.
DAMOND: Simple question, munchkin. Simple answer—negative or affirmative.
JOEL: Check the schedule.
DAMOND: What are you grinnin' at, Cheshire Cat?
JOEL: *(Grinning.)* Nothing.
(ELLY enters with her arms full of groceries. She tries to get past GINA and open the door.)
ELLY: Gina, could you get the door?
GINA: My nails are wet. I just—
ELLY: It's OK. I'll manage.
(ELLY struggles. GINA gets up to help her, while keeping her fingernails extended and away from contact. The struggle becomes comic.)
JOEL: Fact is, Damond, we may not be partners much longer.
DAMOND: "Gracious Lord, you been listenin'!"
JOEL: You may be slingin' "peli-cans" all by your lonesome while I'm…doin' something else.
DAMOND: What's goin' on?
JOEL: Stay tuned, big guy.
GINA: If I use my elbow—
ELLY: Don't ruin your nails—
GINA: No, I got it—*(GINA is positioned such that her face is right over a grocery bag.)* Aw, you buy tomatoes at Giant?
ELLY: What?

GINA: Why don't you go to the Korean market down the street? They got the best prices.

ELLY: I go there sometimes.

DAMOND: Don't mess with me, munchkin.

GINA: *(Calling after ELLY.)* Woo Sung's. Right down the street.

ELLY: I know.

JOEL: I'm planning a move up in the world. Up and out.

GINA: Can you get it?

JOEL: Get it?

ELLY: I got it.

JOEL: Up and out!

(JOEL exits the bus triumphantly, while ELLY enters the apartment defeatedly. DAMOND stomps off the bus, while GINA exits, confused by what she said wrong.)

SCENE EIGHT

DAMOND appears with a telephone. He is at the head office of the recycling company.

DAMOND: Lamont? Hey man, listen up. No, I'm at work. No, I'm not sitting under a tree with my trash can. Lay off, man. I'm at the central office, checkin' out the keys to the future. *(Pause.)* Yeah, I know your future. Listen, Lamont. I got something to do tonight. No, that something's name is not Patrice. I gotta work on…something for my job. *(Pause.)* Give me a break, man! Important stuff comin' down here. *(Pause.)* Cause I don't wanna tell you. Don't want you givin' me any crap. This job's workin' for me, man. Yeah, al'right. Thanks, man.

(DAMOND hangs up the phone and exits.)

SCENE NINE

Sound of the recycling office segues into the sound of pop music. The next day. GINA is at her job at Tower Records.

GINA: Seven, forty-two is your change. Thanks for shopping at Tower. Breaktime for Gina. *(Calling offstage.)* You're on register, Sharell.

(JOEL has entered. GINA sees him.)

GINA: Joel! What're you doin' in the Soul Music?

JOEL: *(Laughing.)* Free country!

GINA: *I* don't listen to Soul Music, so you got *no* business browsing over here.

JOEL: So help me pick out a tape. I'm celebrating.

GINA: What?

JOEL: The internship.

GINA: You got it?

JOEL: Not yet. But I just turned in my application smack on time. My Mom, she reads it over word by word. *(Imitating his mother.)* "Make it perfect. Make me proud."

(They laugh.)

JOEL: It *did* look pretty impressive. The sucker was this thick! I'm gonna be "managing" trash.

GINA: Congratulations—I guess.

JOEL: *(Teasing back.)* I can take it. Not everybody gets turned on by garbage. It takes a special spirit—

GINA: *(Laughing.)* Get out.

JOEL: So when do you get off?

GINA: Not till eight.

JOEL: You walk home alone?

GINA: I'm not scared of the neighborhood.

(Awkward pause.)

JOEL: Stop by soon with the lyrics to that song, OK? I could make you another tape, too. You written any new songs?

GINA: I am workin' on one.

JOEL: It's no problem.

GINA: That'd be so great.

JOEL: I hear you sometimes, y'know.

GINA: Through the kitchen vent, huh. Sorry.

JOEL: No, you're terrific. If I can...be a part of what you're tryin' to do just by making a tape—

(DAMOND enters, playing a loud riff on his saxophone, complete with sunglasses and a can of spray paint in his back pocket.)

DAMOND: Aww, put me in a Pepsi commercial.

GINA: Don't bring that in here.

DAMOND: My sax is my voice, my choice, my means of communication.

(He plays another riff.)

GINA: Go communicate on the sidewalk before you get me in trouble.

DAMOND: You gonna let her treat me like this, Mr. Wizard?

(GINA sees the spraypaint. She takes it out of his back pocket.)

GINA: What've you been doin'? Damond! Spray paint?!

DAMOND: I've been communicatin' visually, too.

JOEL: Are you in a gang?

DAMOND: *(Jumping at JOEL.)* Danger! Jump back!

GINA: He's *not*—

DAMOND: I'm expressin' myself. I keep a stash in the trash on the court, so when the urge strikes to speak, I streak. *(Plays a quick riff of the sax.)* Artist of the street.

GINA: You always gotta do this in front of my friends?

DAMOND: That *you*, hotshot?

JOEL: Yeah.

DAMOND: Well, well.

GINA: Grow up, Damond. Joel…I'll talk to you later.

JOEL: We'll make that tape. All right?

GINA: All right.

JOEL: Later, Damond.

(JOEL exits, sent off by a blast from DAMOND's sax.)

DAMOND: I'd set your sights a little higher, sister dear. He's loser-material. Like every one of them who moves in here, thinks he's gonna be king of the hill—top o' the heap.

GINA: And just what the hell are you doin' to get off the bottom?

DAMOND: Cause I used to screw up, you think I can't get it together?

GINA: You call spray paintin' "together?"

DAMOND: "Recreation," Gina. I'm "recreating" the world the way I see it. I ain't on the bottom no more, so why should I keep quiet about it?

GINA: You'd better keep quiet with that spray paint around Momma. She'd run you out if she knew.

DAMOND: Yeah? What if she knew I was the Collector of the Week at work? Not just this week, but last week, too?

GINA: Why didn't you tell us?

DAMOND: Why didn't you ask.

(Pause.)

GINA: I ask you about work.

DAMOND: No, you ask me about Joel.

GINA: That's not true.

DAMOND: Wrapped up in your little dream world, aren't you. Doesn't matter to you *what* I do, as long as you get what you want.

GINA: What I'm gettin' right now is hurt.

DAMOND: This is a race, Gina. And you are backin' the wrong horse. You're gonna lose bad.

GINA: My break's over.

DAMOND: Sorry to take your time. You be a good girl, now. That's right.

GINA: That's right!

(They stare at each other.)

GINA: Damond…Momma's gettin' off early tonight. Let's all have some supper together—

(DAMOND exits.)

GINA: Damond!

(GINA turns to go back to work.)

SCENE TEN

One week later. Rock-music radio is playing. JOEL, at work, enters carrying both bins. He struggles under their weight. He is not happy.

RADIO: Can you take it? Second straight week of 95 degrees plus! It's another scorcher today. *Everywhere* is hot!

DAMOND: *(Entering.)* Yo, Joel.

JOEL: So he finally shows up. Thank you very much.

DAMOND: You're the champ, man. Don't you wanna fly solo?

JOEL: Thanks for the opportunity. Now pick that crate up.

DAMOND: What?

JOEL: Ye who shows up to work on time, usually gets to be boss.

DAMOND: I had some paper work to do at Central Office.

JOEL: Hope you had some help.

DAMOND: Woo, we're hot today.

JOEL: I'm pissed! It's 98 degrees, a million percent humidity, and you're off screwing around somewhere.

DAMOND: I *said* I had something to do.

JOEL: Yeah? Well, I hope she was cute.

DAMOND: *This*, my man, is a one-way conversation. I'm outta here—call it a "break."

JOEL: You just got here.

DAMOND: *(Using an exaggerated accent.)* Sah-rey, boss. Iz gots ta rest mah stupid head!

(DAMOND exits.)

JOEL: Damond! *(To himself, slinging the bins.)* Lazy...lazy black...*lazy!*

(ELLY has entered the apartment. She is on the phone with her mother.)

ELLY: Lazy. Lazy is what they are, Momma. No, last week, she helped me with my groceries, but then she asks me why I don't shop at the Korean market. What, does she think I'm prejudiced? I can't *understand* them at the Korean market. So now I'm a racist?

(JOEL has now exited with his bins.)

ELLY: No...Momma. I can't visit today. I was there yesterday. I know. I know. I've got an interview this afternoon, and I gotta shop...Mi dispiace, Momma. Domani. Domani. Tomorrow, all right!

(Knock on the door. It is GINA.)

ELLY: I gotta go. I'm sorry, Momma. Addio. *(She hangs up.)* Hold on! *(She opens the door.)*

GINA: Mrs. Cohen! I thought Joel would be here.

ELLY: He's working a double shift. My son works very hard.

GINA: I can come back.

ELLY: Can I...tell him anything?

GINA: Could you give this to him? *(She hands ELLY an envelope.)* He'll understand.

ELLY: All right.

GINA: It's the words—

ELLY: You don't have to tell me. My son has his own life. This I understand.

GINA: Thanks.

(GINA exits.)

ELLY: Bye, Gina.

(ELLY holds the note for a moment, she puts it down, then quickly opens it.)

ELLY: "A place...like in my dreams. Where we could go. No one would know. Love..."

(ELLY crumples the note up, and throws it on the floor. She exits.)

SCENE ELEVEN

Four days later. GINA enters the basketball court. She is dribbling the ball. DAMOND enters. She stops, and looks at DAMOND. Then she passes the ball to him. DAMOND passes it back. GINA tries again. This time DAMOND catches it, then drives past her playfully and goes up for an impressive shot.

GINA: I was gonna beat the fire outta you today. What're you in such a good mood for?

DAMOND: *(Exaggerated.)* I've found inner peace.

(GINA hurls the basketball at his stomach. He catches it with a thud.)

DAMOND: And outer drive!

(DAMOND drives the basketball around the court, with GINA in hot pursuit. As he goes up for a basket, JOEL enters.)

JOEL: *(Fake jovial.)* So, there he is.

GINA: *(Passing the ball to JOEL.)* All right. Two-on-one. Come on, Joel.

JOEL: *(Hurling the ball at DAMOND.)* Where you been, Damond?

DAMOND: Say what?

GINA: Joel, what's wrong?

JOEL: Two days I've covered for you. This is it, man.

GINA: You not goin' to work?

JOEL: I'm sick of this! Tomorrow, if I don't see you by 9:01, that's it. I'm reporting you. You've been dumpin' on me all summer.

GINA: *(To DAMOND.)* You said you were doin' so good.

DAMOND: I'm doin' fine.

JOEL: That's a joke.

DAMOND: No, the *joke* is that I *have* been at work. Thought you had it nailed, didn't you. Thought you were the only one smart and slick enough. Well, meet the Recycling Center Summer Management Intern. Check it out.

GINA: When'd you find out?

DAMOND: Yesterday.

JOEL: We were supposed to be personally notified.

DAMOND: Bulletin board not personal enough for you?

JOEL: I thought I'd get a letter.

DAMOND: Well you thought wrong. Congratulate me, Gina. I've jumped to the front of the movie line, bought my ticket, and I'm watchin' from the front row.

JOEL: There's no way you're qualified. You never graduated.

DAMOND: I got my GED and experience. You ever had a job before this one?

JOEL: No.

DAMOND: I've had two.

JOEL: But you were fired, right?

DAMOND: I quit—

JOEL: Right.

DAMOND: Cause they weren't jobs. They were "opportunities" that'd be gone as soon as some fat-cat bureaucrat decided to reshuffle the deck.

JOEL: Well, you were dealt a great hand on this one.

DAMOND: That's right. Cry poor. Cry poor little white guy. That's bull, man. I got this because I worked for it. I worked hard. Just cause I didn't waste any time tryin' to prove something to *you*, you think I don't deserve it.

JOEL: *I* deserved it.

DAMOND: Yeah, you might. But this time around, there was only one showin' of the movie. Life's hell, man.

GINA: *(To JOEL.)* You can try next time—

JOEL: Wouldn't waste my time.

GINA: Joel—

JOEL: Why should I? I gotta be black to get a break around here.

DAMOND: You dumb enough to think that? Then hit the road, Jack. Why don't you and your Momma take forty days and forty night and wander back to the promised land.

GINA: Damond!

DAMOND: You're like any other Jew-boy. Can't see past your nose.

JOEL: Just get me away from lazy black-asses like you.

GINA: Both of you—

DAMOND: Always snappin' at my heels like a spoiled puppy. Head back to Jew-land. Kike-berg!

JOEL: Bastard! Black bas—

(DAMOND pushes JOEL. JOEL pushes him back.)

GINA: Stop it.

DAMOND: I'm not even gonna bother to bust your face. You're not worth it.

(He begins to exit.)

GINA: Joel, go inside. There's no point—

DAMOND: Go on, little boy. Momma's callin'. Your girlfriend's bawlin'—

GINA: I'll come over. We'll play some music. D'you get the note I left for you?

JOEL: Leave me alone. Both of you. Leave me alone!

(JOEL exits toward his apartment.)

GINA: Joel!

DAMOND: Writin' love notes to the Kike?

GINA: Don't say those words around me.

DAMOND: Awwh. My sweet, gentle sister.

GINA: Stop it. Shut up!

(GINA exits. DAMOND crosses out after her.)

SCENE TWELVE

ELLY is waiting for JOEL as he enters his apartment.

ELLY: I expected you home sooner. I've waited dinner.
   (JOEL does not reply. He paces silently.)
ELLY: So how's your grandmother? Joel?
JOEL: What?
ELLY: Your grandmother.
JOEL: What about her?
ELLY: You forgot.
JOEL: What?
ELLY: Today. Today you were supposed to visit your grandmother.
JOEL: I forgot.
ELLY: How could you? Three days and no visits from us. She's lonely. I'm try-
   ing to study—
JOEL: I'm sorry.
ELLY: Where were you?
   (No reply.)
ELLY: Answer me when I ask you a question.
JOEL: Nowhere.
ELLY: You can't be nowhere. You have to be somewhere.
JOEL: Nowhere different.
ELLY: You're not telling me the truth. My son is lying to me. What else? What
   else do you need to tell me.
   (JOEL ignores her.)
ELLY: You used to be here every night. Now you're not. What are you doing?
   Who are you seeing?
JOEL: What are you talking about?
ELLY: This is my house. My rules.
JOEL: What rules? Thou shalt abide by thy mother's moods? Thou shalt sort
   through garbage like a pig while Mother studies for a test she'll probably
   never take?
   (GINA and DAMOND enter their apartment. The scenes overlap.)
DAMOND: You think of me like he does, don't you?
GINA: Don't put me in the middle of this.
DAMOND: You and Momma been harpin' on me to make something of
   myself. Now I've done it and you don't give a damn.
JOEL: Your rules make as much sense as that lazy-ass getting a job over me!

ELLY: You lost? You lost the internship? What's wrong with them! Can't they see you're made to be a manager! Not some shlep on a truck.

JOEL: I couldn't always keep up, OK?!

GINA: I'm proud of you, Damond—

DAMOND: But you "feel sorry" for Joel.

ELLY: How could you miss this opportunity? I thought this was important to you?

GINA: I can feel whatever I want.

DAMOND: Fallin' for a wimp-ass kike—

(DAMOND grabs GINA's tape out of her boom box.)

ELLY: Or have you been too busy going out with *black* girls.

GINA: Don't.

(DAMOND hurls the tape at GINA. She scrambles to retrieve it.)

JOEL: Shut up!

ELLY: Get out!

(JOEL runs from the apartment. All other characters freeze. A pulsing, pounding music starts. JOEL runs on, stopping center. DAMOND and ELLY shift to frozen positions within the playing area. GINA exits.

JOEL is breathless, fueled by a level of anger he has never experienced before. He "runs" through the neighborhood. He confronts the frozen DAMOND and ELLY during the sequence.)

JOEL: Out…I'll get out…I'll hit the road, Damond. See? I know my way 'round too. On the right…we have windows…windows. *(He hurls a stone through a window. Sound of shattering glass.)* No more window! On the left…no more crap…from *you!* (He hurls another stone. Another window shatters.) From any of you. Lazy bastards. All of you. *(He hurls a final stone, shattering a window. Now JOEL is back on the basketball court. He sees the trash can.)* And here…Damond. Manage some trash! *(JOEL dumps out the contents of the trash can. He sees the can of spray paint.)* I'll speak. Streak. Speak…

(JOEL begins to spray paint over and over again. GINA runs on. She is clutching the tape. She stops dead. She sees what JOEL has written. They stare at one another in horrible silence. Finally, GINA speaks.)

GINA: Me?

JOEL: No…

GINA: Me!

JOEL: Gina…

(JOEL cannot speak. He runs from the court. GINA turns to face the graffiti-covered wall.)

GINA: Nigger. Nigger trash. Nigger trash. Trash! Nigger *trash!*
(*She cries, almost buckling under the pain. A police siren sounds. GINA is now still and silent, still clutching the tape. She faces downstage. ELLY and DAMOND rush in. They are both talking downstage, separately, as if to a policeman.*)
ELLY: I heard broken glass.
DAMOND: Broken, man. Why don't you *do* something.
ELLY: He was upset. He could be hurt.
DAMOND: Why do we have to *look* at this.
ELLY: Help me.
DAMOND: Why?
ELLY: Help me! I don't know where he is. I was angry—
DAMOND: Yeah, I'm angry—
ELLY: He was angry…What's happened?
DAMOND: My sister.
ELLY: What's happened?
DAMOND: She'll never forget—
ELLY: What's happened to us?!
DAMOND: Those words…inside her forever.
ELLY: Joel, why like this?
DAMOND: Words…Hate.
ELLY: Joel.
DAMOND: Gina.
(*DAMOND and ELLY freeze. A single piano line plays slowly, erratically, the final lines from GINA's song, "The Other Side of Now." GINA holds the cassette tape, and slowly begins to pull the tape from its plastic. She unwinds it slowly, pulling out longer, arm's-length pieces. It is tangled around her arms. The piano music stops. She slowly, almost ritualistically, lays it on the ground. ELLY and DAMOND exit. GINA, alone, looks at the tape, then exits.*)

END OF PLAY

Blessings

FOR WHITNEY

Whitney Couch as Rene and Bob Green as Jesse in Blessings,
California Theatre Center, 1990. Photo by California Theatre Center.

ORIGINAL PRODUCTION

Blessings opened at Weisiger Theatre, Centre College, Danville, Kentucky, on February 2, 1994. The director was Anthony Haigh, the set designer was Mark deAraujo, the lighting designer was Camille Davis, the costumer was Allison Anderson, the sound design and original music was by Mary Hall Surface. The stage manager was Ashley Ducker. The cast was as follows:

RENE . . . . Jenifer Ducker
MAGGIE . . . . Anna Goodman
RANDY . . . . Brandon Heringer
CHARLIE . . . . Andrew MacGregor
ANGELA . . . . Julie Shankle
KATIE . . . . Lisa Dixon
JESSE . . . . Jason Reed

An earlier version of the play, *The Mixed Blessings,* was produced by the California Theatre Center in January, 1990, under the direction of Graham Whitehead.

Blessings was a finalist at the 1996 Waldo M. and Grace C. Bonderman IUPUI National Youth Theatre Playwriting Workshop.

NOTES FOR *BLESSINGS*

The idea for *Blessings* happened before I knew I was a playwright. It was during my first summer with the California Theatre Center (CTC), two years after I graduated from Centre College. As part of our Summer Conservatory program, I was teaching a creative writing class. The mother of one of my students, a doe-eyed eight-year-old named Whitney, told me, "Just don't ask Whitney to read anything out loud in front of the group. Otherwise, she's fine." This learning-disabled child was more than fine. She was one of the most imaginative, spontaneous, genuinely playful kids in the bunch. I loved her.

One day, we were writing poems, inspired by images from Shakespeare (Whitney was one of Titania's most inspired fairies). The energy in the room was high. The kids were excited by this task and revelled in new word play. When it came time to read, hands shot into the air. After a few poems were read, I noticed Whitney's hand go up. "Good for me, I thought. Even Whitney is willing to try." "You next, Whitney," I said. Her older brother, also in the class, looked strangely panicked. Whitney slowly stands up. I'm thinking, "She *wrote* this. *Of course* she can read it." But as the first few words slipped tentatively, tortuously from her lips, I realized how dead wrong I was. I stammer, "It's OK, Whitney." But she won't quit. Any giggles from the classroom disappear. She struggles and cries and struggles. Her brother, at her side in a shot, helps her get through it, arm around her, sounding out the words. And I sit like a lump on the desk at the front of the classroom.

This memory still stings. My ignorance was perhaps understandable; my inability to stop the avalanche of pain and embarrassment was not. It was five years later, when Whitney had grown into a fine young actress, one of the few young people used in our professional productions, that her mother approached me. "You've got to write a play about her, Mary Hall Surface. About what it's like to be so blessed, and so cursed at once. People have to understand." That was the real beginning.

Born as *The Mixed Blessings,* the play was originally conceived as an hour-long piece intended for a fourth to eighth grade audience, and their families. It opened in 1990, and performed for three weeks at CTC. Rene was played by (can you guess?)—Whitney. Katie was played by another long-time student—a child who equally fascinated me. How could "Katie" be so bright, so accomplished, so acknowledged, and yet often seem so deeply unhappy? It took the inspiration of both young women to give the play its form.

If we're lucky, the beginning idea for us playwrights twists and turns and mutates and develops into something larger—something that can hold our passions and hopes and fears, and sing them out loud and clear. I have always been driven to encourage adults and young people to see one another afresh—in new light. *Blessings,* the play's new incarnation, looks at questions of parenting and childing, of being lost and being found all in one weekend in the Santa Cruz mountains. While all of us are not faced every day by Rene's challenges—severe dyslexia and auditory perception deficit—we *are* all blessed and cursed by who we are, and, just as importantly, by what others *think* we are.

—*Mary Hall Surface*

CHARACTERS

RENE: Fourteen-year-old freshman in high school, a watercolorist, has severe
    dyslexia and an auditory perception deficit
MAGGIE: Thirty-six years old, Rene's Mother
RANDY: Thirty-eight years old, Maggie's brother, recent owner of the cabin
CHARLIE: Thirty-eight years old, Randy's best friend in high school
ANGELA: Thirty years old, Charlie's girfriend
KATIE: Fourteen-year-old freshman in high school, Charlie's daughter, an
    excellent student, very talented musically, a perfectionist
JESSE: Twenty-nine years old. Lives in the basement apartment of the cabin.
    His parents were the cabin's original owners. He is a craftsman, making
    redwood-frame mirrors. Unknown to all, he has severe dyslexia.

SETTING

A cabin in the Santa Cruz mountains of California and an outcropping of rock
that forms an overlook high above the valley below and to the ocean beyond.

TIME

October, 1990

SCENE ONE

A late Friday afternoon in mid-October. LIGHTS UP, isolating RENE, sitting at the window of a rustic mountain cabin. She is painting with watercolors.

RENE: Pigments. Reds and yellows from clay. Colored clay. Black from burnt wood. Each ground into dust. Water from a river. Comfort. Paint on the walls of caves. Birds. Stickmen dancing. Fire! Pictures of the day. Storydreams. Trying to speak. To know. What's outside the cave? Animals bigger than you, caveman. Inside? You thought you knew, but do you? Don't hide! Follow the map of pictures. Pictures to the *outside*. Take a step. Go on. Don't be afraid. Put one foot in front of another. Left foot, right foot, left foot...left foot...
(RENE's musings are invaded by a memory. A six-year-old KATIE appears, separate, isolated in light.)

KATIE: Left foot, right foot, both feet, right foot, left foot, both feet, right jump, turn—Can't you even play hopscotch?

RENE: *(To herself.)* I...

KATIE: I'm the hopscotch champion.

RENE: Right foot, left foot...which foot?

KATIE: Don't you know which foot is which?

RENE: *(Pulling herself out of the memory.)* Both feet. Follow the map of colors. Inside. Which colors...?
(LIGHTS UP, returning to realism, on the full room as RENE's mother, MAGGIE, and her uncle, RANDY, enter. The cabin has a warm, rustic interior. An upstage door leads to the porch. Another door leads to a hallway to the bedrooms. The main room has a couch, a wood-burning stove, a desk, a dining table and chairs, bookcases, and an old upright piano, and a very basic kitchen.)

RANDY: *(Bursting through the front door, carrying a few groceries.)* Success. *Love* that market at the bottom of the hill.

MAGGIE: *(Staggering under the weight of more groceries.)* These qualify as mountains, you maniac.

RANDY: What, sis, just a few hairpin turns.

MAGGIE: At sixty miles an hour! You were smart to stay here, Rene.

RANDY: *(To RENE.)* So whaddya think of my home-away-from-home? Been checkin' things out?

RENE: I was water coloring.

RANDY: Lemme see.

RENE: *(Closing her sketch pad.)* I didn't finish. Show you later.

RANDY: Whatever you say. When's Charlie supposed to get here, Mags?

MAGGIE: *(Putting away groceries.)* Depends on traffic.

RANDY: Man, a guy should never go eight years without seein' his best buddy from high school.

MAGGIE: *(To RENE.)* Want a coke, or some juice?

RANDY: What happens to us?

RENE: No thanks, Mom.

RANDY: Why do we lose touch?

MAGGIE: Maybe we grow up.

RANDY: Do *not* accuse me of that! *(To RENE.)* Quiz time. Santa Clara High School, 1972. Charlie, #24; yours truly, #18. We were…

RENE: Basketball stars.

RANDY: See, this kid doesn't have any trouble remembering the important stuff, do you, little one.

RENE: *Nobody* calls me that anymore.

RANDY: Sure, no problem… *(Teasing her.)* doodle bug.

RENE: Uncle Randy!

MAGGIE: Rene's a *freshman* this year.

RANDY: A high schooler! So, how's it goin'?

(MAGGIE tunes in even more carefully than she already has been to any signals RENE's response might give.)

RENE: It's going.

MAGGIE: You've got a couple of classes you like. *(No reply.)* Honey?

RENE: Couple.

MAGGIE: Your study skills class—

(RENE crosses away from them, but RANDY pursues her.)

RANDY: Blow it off for the weekend, Van Gogh. Look at all these mountains waitin' for you to paint or hike. Anything you want.

RENE: *(At the window.)* I like the light in the trees. Looks like fingers. Are those…redwoods yours, too?

RANDY: They're Jesse's. He grew up in this cabin. Spent his whole life right here on this mountain. He takes care of all of it for me when I'm not here.

MAGGIE: Jesse here this weekend?

RANDY: Whaddya mean? He never leaves. Ever.

RENE: Can we go to the meadow? With the wildflowers?

RANDY: Now you're talkin'. I've got it all mapped out. Weekend hiking goal: 25.4 miles. God, I love the mountains!

MAGGIE: "25.4?"

RANDY: Aren't you comin', sis?

MAGGIE: I got tired of following after you when I was ten.

RENE: I'll wike...*hike*, if I can stop and pick wildflowers.

RANDY: Deal.

MAGGIE: Charlie could be here any time. We gotta all be here to welcome them.

RENE: Them?

MAGGIE: Charlie's new girlfriend—Angela, remember?

RANDY: The new *amour*. Hey, what about his kid?

MAGGIE: Katie? She spends weekends with her Mom.

RENE: *(Under her breath.)* Thank God.

MAGGIE: Rene.

RANDY: Oooo. Juicy stuff, huh? You two little girls not get along so well last reunion time? What'd she do? Pull one of your pigtails? Throw one of your Barbies off a cliff?

RENE: *(Insightfully.)* Why is everything a joke to you?

RANDY: *(Taken aback.)* Just keepin' things light. That's my job.

MAGGIE: Want to walk to the meadow, honey? I'll go—

RENE: I'll go.

MAGGIE: But—

RANDY: You can do it. Take a left at the bottom of the drive, then follow the road to where we turned in. Remember the sign?

RENE: *(She doesn't.)* Yeah.

RANDY: The trail head is right there. Walk a quarter a mile up and there it'll be.

MAGGIE: Sure you don't want me to come?

RENE: *(Leaving.)* I'm fine.

RANDY: She's fine. *(RENE exits.)*

MAGGIE: Bravo, big brother. *(Mimicking him.)* "I know kids. Let *me* talk to her."

RANDY: Gimme time. Put some wood in the stove, will ya?

(MAGGIE goes over somewhat tentatively to the wood basket, then carries pieces to the wood-burning stove. As she becomes more agitated, she stuffs more and more wood into the stove.)

MAGGIE: I just don't get it. She fades in and out of being who I know. She's never closed up like this. Talking to each other—that's how we've survived.

RANDY: This is a "get-away" cabin, Mags. Leave it back in San Raphael.

MAGGIE: And just watch her while she sinks or swims? She doesn't know anybody. It's the first time she's been mainstreamed. She walked into that high school and they stuck a label on her forehead—"learning impaired."

RANDY: You're kidding!

MAGGIE: Well, they might as well have! She's not coping.

RANDY: *(Rushing over to stop her.)* Maggie, what are you building? The towering inferno? That's plenty.

MAGGIE: Sorry.

RANDY: *You* are not coping, Mags. Little one's fine.

MAGGIE: You don't know that. You only see her three or four times a year, if we're lucky.

RANDY: Hey, I got this weekend together, didn't I? It's working out well, givin' Rene *and* you some escape time? *(He hugs her.)* Come on, sis, this weekend was supposed to be about me. *Everything* is about me.

(They laugh. Then RENE bursts back through the door, triumphant. She has a big, beautiful bunch of wildflowers.)

RENE: Look!

RANDY: A successful safari.

RENE: I found these by the road. I'll go to the meadow later.

MAGGIE: They're beautiful.

RENE: *(Describing the flowers.)* Gold, and a water-green.

MAGGIE: And violet.

RENE: Blue-violet. Vase. Quick.

(RANDY jumps comically to the rescue.)

RENE: It's beautiful up here, Mom. Smells cool, kinda wet.

MAGGIE: You like it, sunshine?

RANDY: We're right next to a state park. The trails, they scream at me, "Hike me, hike me."

(RENE and MAGGIE laugh. Randy produces a vase.)

RANDY: How's this?

RENE: It's got to be *right*, for the flowers. That's not.

RANDY: Picky, picky.

RENE: *(Enjoying herself.)* I'm an *artist!*

MAGGIE: *(Taking a vase off the bookshelf.)* How's this?

RENE: It fits.

(RENE goes into the kitchen to put the flowers in water. RANDY crosses to the table, pulls big hiking maps out of his backpack, and spreads them out on the table.)

RENE: I'll give them to…her. Charlie's…

MAGGIE: Angela?

RENE: Angela. She'll need to feel welcome.

(MAGGIE smiles at RENE's insight.)

RANDY: *(Finding what he was looking for on the map.)* Here we go. The white and the blue trails go across the ridge.

MAGGIE: *(Crossing to map.)* Which ones?

RANDY: One hundred and eighty degree views from some spots. Come look, Rene.

RENE: You can just tell me where we're gonna hike.

RANDY: Come on! I need an assistant scout.

MAGGIE: Randy…

RENE: I don't like those maps—

RANDY: This lists the difficulty of the blue trail as medium. Medium? That's for wimps!

(Suddenly there is the sound of a car horn outside, honking exuberantly.)

MAGGIE: *(Jumping up.)* That's *got* to be Charlie.

RANDY: *(Heading for the door.)* Yo, crazy Charlie!

(RENE is relieved not to have to interpret the map. MAGGIE and RANDY cross to the door, and fling it open to reveal a smiling CHARLIE with his arms open wide.)

MAGGIE: Charlie!

CHARLIE: Hey, hey, hey!

(The following lines are rapid and overlapping. Everyone is talking at once and hugging.)

MAGGIE: Look at you! You look as wonderful as ever. San Diego must be good to you. How have you been?

RANDY: You ole geezer! Still crazy after all these years? How ya been? Still shooting the hoops?

CHARLIE: Maggie, you little beauty. You haven't changed a bit. Randy, what happened? You haven't gotten old and ugly like me! *(After bubbling over each other, CHARLIE strikes a pose, then the others join in.)* Two bits.

MAGGIE and CHARLIE: Four bits.

RANDY, CHARLIE, and MAGGIE: Six bits, a dollar. All for the Panthers, stand up and holler.

(They all let out a "holler," then laugh. ANGELA appears at the door with a heavy garment bag.)

ANGELA: Charlie, you didn't tell me you were a cheerleader in high school.

CHARLIE: We're just being crazy, sweetheart.

CHARLIE and RANDY: As usual.

CHARLIE: Maggie, Randy, this is Angela Thompson.

ANGELA: Nice to meet you. I've heard so much about you.

MAGGIE: Welcome.

RANDY: Charlie, she's beautiful. *(To ANGELA.)* How'd you get stuck with an old guy like this?

ANGELA: *(Laughing.)* Just lucky, I guess.

MAGGIE: And *this* is Rene.

CHARLIE: Look at you. The last time I saw you, you were this high! You're gonna be breakin' hearts in no time, just like your Mom.

ANGELA: We really appreciate the invitation, Randy.

RANDY: Gotta show off my new digs!

MAGGIE: I can't believe it's really you, Charlie.

CHARLIE: Well, it's me.

KATIE: *(From porch.)* What about me?!

CHARLIE: I almost blew the surprise. Close your eyes, Rene.

(Rene stands still. She does not close her eyes, turn her back, anything.)

CHARLIE: Oh, come on. You're not too big to play a little game. Close your eyes!

KATIE: *(Entering.)* Surprise.

CHARLIE: *(Disappointed.)* Katie!

KATIE: I didn't want to wait anymore.

CHARLIE: Rene, you remember Katie.

RENE: Yeah.

CHARLIE: We talked Katie's mother out of her for the weekend, just so you two girls could be together.

ANGELA: *(Putting her arm around KATIE.)* And us two girls.

KATIE: *(Moving away from ANGELA.)* Hi Rene.

RENE: Hi.

ANGELA: Isn't this wonderful? Now everyone has a friend for the weekend.

MAGGIE: Well…

RANDY: *Well,* come on in everybody.

(Everybody moves toward the couch and chairs. RENE keeps her distance.)

MAGGIE: Katie, you're so grown up.

KATIE: Thank you.

RANDY: She's pretty, Charlie.

KATIE: *(To RANDY.)* I remember you from Dad's yearbooks, I think.

RANDY: And *smart*, too!

KATIE: I'm glad you've got a piano. I need to practice.

ANGELA: Katie, this is vacation.

(KATIE crosses to the piano. She plays a few scales.)

RANDY: Whoa, she's good. *(To KATIE.)* Hey, you like to hike?

ANGELA: I haven't been on a real hike in years! I don't know if I can make it up anything too steep!

KATIE: I could.

CHARLIE: You can do anything you want, sweetheart. Why I bet you'll beat everybody to the top of the mountain.

MAGGIE: Rene, don't you have something for Angela? *(RENE is still. MAGGIE hints to her.)* Gold and blue-violet?

(RENE crosses to the flowers.)

ANGELA: Ooo, I love surprises.

(RENE gives ANGELA the flowers.)

ANGELA: Aren't they cute! And aren't you a sweetie to buy them for me!

RENE: I picked them.

ANGELA: How nice of you.

RANDY: Shoulda gotten some flowers for Katie, Rene.

RENE: I didn't know she was coming.

KATIE: Well, I did. *(Smiles at RENE.)* So, what happens first?

RANDY: I have got the most spectacular place to watch the sunset.

ANGELA: I bet it's beautiful from up here. Charlie, let's—

KATIE: *(Reaches for her Dad first.)* Come on, Dad.

CHARLIE: Sounds good.

(All begin to exit, except RENE. The following lines come rapidly, overlapping.)

ANGELA: Should we get our things unpacked first?

RANDY: Later! Race ya to the blue trail!

CHARLIE: Walk, buddy, walk.

ANGELA: Do we need jackets?

MAGGIE: I don't think so. *(Noticing that RENE has not budged.)* Rene, aren't you coming?

RENE: I'll catch up. I want to shoes my change—*(Slowly, correcting herself.)* *Change* my *shoes.*

KATIE: Can I help you find them?

RENE: I know where they are.

MAGGIE: But you don't know which trail to follow.

RENE: Yes I do.

MAGGIE: Look for the blue markings on the trees.

KATIE: You can follow the colors.

(RENE looks at KATIE as if she has invaded her private painter's world.)

MAGGIE: Are you sure you—

RENE: I can *do* this, Mom. Go on.

(*MAGGIE and KATIE exit. RENE pauses and looks around the cabin, as if for an escape route. But finally, she takes a deep breath, and begins to look for her shoes.*)

RENE: If I were shoes, where would I be?

(*RENE searches her Mom's bag, under the couch. Her exasperation builds. She cannot remember where they are. Frustrated she yells at herself.*)

RENE: Why can't you remember, stupid! Stupid brain! Stupid broken brain!

(*RENE hurls a pillow from the couch across the room just as JESSE enters the cabin. He is carrying a stack of firewood.*)

JESSE: Oh. I didn't think anybody was here.

RENE: They're not.

JESSE: Aren't you somebody?

RENE: Well, yeah. Sorry. I'm Rene.

JESSE: Jesse.

RENE: I thought so.

JESSE: Nice to meet you.

(*Awkward pause. Then JESSE crosses over to firewood basket. RENE crosses to retrieve the pillow.*)

JESSE: Got to make sure we got plenty of wood for you folks. Usually just Randy up here on the weekends. Just me the rest of the time.

RENE: You like living up here?

JESSE: Wouldn't live anywhere else.

RENE: You must like being alone.

JESSE: Yeah, I guess I do.

RENE: I wish I could be alone.

JESSE: (*Hurrying.*) Be done in a second. Just stockin' the wood.

RENE: I—

JESSE: Then the place's all yours. Don't like bein' in the way.

RENE: Wait. I didn't mean…I'm sorry, I'm just…I don't know.

JESSE: You're what.

RENE: I don't know.

JESSE: Well, you're how old?

RENE: Fourteen.

JESSE: You run around with friends. Phone calls. Parties.

RENE: I'm different for my age.

JESSE: Are ya? (*RENE nods.*) You proud of that?

RENE: (*Thinking about KATIE.*) Usually.

JESSE: So. Where'd everybody go?

RENE: To watch the sunset.

JESSE: You don't like sunsets?

RENE: I wanted to be by myself.

JESSE: Tell you what. I've got this place. It's not mine. It belongs to the mountain, but I lay claim to it sometimes. My "looking spot." I go there to be by myself and...to look.

RENE: At what?

JESSE: Anything. Can see clear across to the next ridge.

RENE: You go there a lot?

JESSE: When I want to look out. And when I want to look...the other way.

RENE: Can I go there?

JESSE: Have to take you the first time. It's tricky.

RENE: Let's go.

JESSE: Now?

RENE: Right now. Please.

JESSE: "Rene," right? *(RENE nods.)* We'll see a sunset nobody else will see. Come on.

(They exit. LIGHTS OUT. Music transition.)

SCENE TWO

LIGHTS UP on the "looking spot," an outcropping of rock on the peak of a ridge, high above the valley below. JESSE is leading the way. They are just arriving.

JESSE: *(Entering.)* It gets cooler, brighter, right at the bend. See?

RENE: *(Entering.)* And thinner. The air feels thinner.

JESSE: Cause it is.

(RENE reaches the top. She looks out for the first time.)

RENE: Oh my *gosh.*

JESSE: Like it?

RENE: I didn't know sunsets came like this! How high *are* we?

JESSE: High as you can get without ropes. See that ridge? Sheer rock-face. I scale that once a year. Since I was twelve. It's my test.

RENE: Are those little color specks houses?

JESSE: Ben Lomand. And that way, if the fog's up, you can see the ocean and the lighthouse from Seal Rock, flickering, kinda like a heartbeat.

RENE: How'd you find this?

JESSE: Sniffed it out. *(RENE laughs.)* All right. Review. First turn?

RENE: When you smell the *(Proud of remembering.)* "eucalyptus," follow the smell.

JESSE: Good. Next turn.

RENE: At the tallest redwood with the…uh…

JESSE: Burl. Think curl. Wood curling.

RENE: *Burl* that looks like a big bump on a giant nose. Then follow the nose.

JESSE: Until—

RENE: You see the blue-gray rock. Then straight up the trail, carpeted with "golden orange-brown" needles, sniffing the air cool. Watch the trees for bright, then Tah-dah!

JESSE: Great map, huh?

RENE: The best! *(RENE crosses to have a seat neat the edge.)* Jeez!!

JESSE: Careful. There's no map for gettin' you back up if you fall.

RENE: Sorry.

(They settle into sitting.)

RENE: Man, I've got to bring my paints up here.

JESSE: You paint?

RENE: Watercolor.

JESSE: What of?

RENE: Maps. Picture maps. Of places. Uncle Randy says *you* make amazing mirrors. From redwood.

JESSE: Don't know how amazing they are. But I make 'em. And sell 'em. So people can see themselves in the—through the wood.

RENE: What else do you do?

JESSE: Like to cook. Like poems. Ever written a poem?

RENE: I don't do poems. Too many words. Is that a river?

JESSE: Runs all the way to the ocean. I hike the whole length of it. Ever seen where a river and the ocean meet?

RENE: I'm not sure.

JESSE: Down at Sunset Beach. You can see it flow clear down the mountain 'til it forms a riverbed right on the beach, in the sand. The water looks real clear. Light. Not like the ocean at all. Like it's not really supposed to be there, but it is. Then the waves just lap up and catch it, little bit at a time. Then it all changes.

RENE: What's it like having Uncle Randy live in your house?

(JESSE looks at RENE, surprised by her directness.)

RENE: Do you wish he'd go away? That it could be all yours again?

JESSE: Don't know how I'm supposed to answer that.

(RENE waits for an answer.)

JESSE: Rene, I've spent a lot of days, nights, too, wishin' that things weren't the way they are. But yeah. I wish I'd never had to sell the cabin and all you people had stayed back in San Francisco—

RENE: San Raphael.

JESSE: Takes away the pattern. New rhythm—gets me off beat.

RENE: *(Getting up.)* I should head back now.

JESSE: Rene—

RENE: I just do the map backwards, right?

JESSE: Rene, wait. Please don't think…I'm not used to lots of new people. I'm not…wanting to be a…I don't know.

RENE: *(Enjoying repeating what he said to her.)* A what?

JESSE: *(Enjoying it, too.)* I don't know.

RENE: You've got stranger-invasion.

JESSE: *(Laughs.)* Will it kill me?

RENE: I don't like them either. Strangers.

JESSE: What *do* you like?

RENE: Being by myself. I understand me when everybody else is lost. *(JESSE laughs.)* Let's go back.

JESSE: Rene, first, would you read this? *(JESSE takes a piece of paper out of his shirt pocket. He hands it to RENE.)* It's a poem. Real short. I wrote it about this place.

RENE: *(Glancing at the page.)* It's nice.

JESSE: No, aloud. I need to hear it.

RENE: I…I'll read it later, Jesse. After dinner. You're gonna eat with us, aren't you?

(JESSE nods.)

RENE: Great! Now, sniffin' for that needle carpet.

JESSE: *(As they exit, playfully.)* They're "yellow" orange-brown, you know.

RENE: *Golden* orange-brown!

JESSE: *(Laughing.)* Whatever!

(RENE and JESSE exit. LIGHTS OUT. Music transition.)

SCENE THREE

Friday night, about 11:00 PM. LIGHTS UP on everyone gathered in the main room of the cabin. RENE is sitting at the desk, painting. JESSE is sitting slightly away from the group, but he is listening to their stories. KATIE is sitting right in the middle of everything.

MAGGIE: *(Over much laughter.)* We had to have been crazy to do that!

CHARLIE: Do you remember the all-district basketball tournament our junior year?

RANDY: I still dream about that cheerleader from Monterey.

CHARLIE: Marlene!

RANDY: Where are you today, Marlene?

MAGGIE: She married the drum major—Bart Jenkins.

CHARLIE and RANDY: *(Disgusted.)* Bart Jenkins??!!

RANDY: What a loss!

MAGGIE: Wasn't that was the same year you won student council president, Charlie?

CHARLIE: *(Tragically.)* Vice-president.

MAGGIE: How *could* I forget. Sorry.

ANGELA: Maggie, Charlie said you were voted outstanding English student every year of your life!

MAGGIE: Almost every year!

ANGELA: Were you a writer, or just a reader?

MAGGIE: A writer.

KATIE: So you're an author?

MAGGIE: Used to be.

ANGELA: Well, who has time for anything *extra* these days.

CHARLIE: Katie, tell 'em what *you* won this year.

KATIE: Dad!

CHARLIE: President of the freshman class!

RANDY: Way to go.

MAGGIE: Congratulations.

KATIE: Thank you.

ANGELA: Katie's involved in so many activities at school I can't keep them straight.

KATIE: It's hard for *me* to keep them straight.

ANGELA: But she does, and we are so proud of her.

JESSE: Katie, what's your favorite subject?

KATIE: I'm best in math.

JESSE: What do you *like* the best?

KATIE: *(Genuinely not sure.)* I don't know.

CHARLIE: Come on, sweetheart.

KATIE: I like reading, and writing—poetry, especially.

RANDY: Hey, Jesse's a poet!

ANGELA: Really?!

JESSE: Just a beginner.

ANGELA: I loved poetry in high school. I'd memorize all those beautiful words, and say them over and over. I dreamed that someday, somebody would "compare me to a summer's day." Never happened. *(To KATIE.)* We should read some together sometime, Sweetie. *(KATIE turns away.)*

CHARLIE: Tell 'em about your latest project.

KATIE: Dad!

CHARLIE: Why can't I brag?

RANDY: Out with it, Katie.

KATIE: I'm in this honors class in music. We have to write fifteen songs, music *and* words, by the end of the quarter.

CHARLIE: She'll do it!

RANDY: How'd you end up with this whiz kid? You never made above a "C+" in your life.

ANGELA: *(Giggling.)* Were you one of the dumb kids?

(RENE and MAGGIE bristle. JESSE checks for RENE's reaction.)

CHARLIE: I was smart as a whip. Just never gave two bits for studying.

ANGELA: *(To RENE.)* Do you…have a favorite subject, Rene?

RENE: In school?

ANGELA: Well, yes. *(In a loud whisper to CHARLIE.)* She's in a real school, isn't she?

(CHARLIE nods that he thinks so.)

RENE: *(Topping the whispering.)* I like art.

MAGGIE: Rene's a watercolorist.

ANGELA: *(Crossing to RENE at desk.)* So that's what you're working away on. Let's see.

RENE: I haven't finished this one.

ANGELA: I *love* pretty pictures. *(She picks up the painting. She is amazed, genuinely impressed.)* Oh. This is wonderful.

RENE: It's abstract—emotional.

ANGELA: It's lovely. I didn't know you could—

KATIE: My paintings are *really* abstract. You can never tell what they are.

(KATIE picks up one of RENE's paintings and looks at it. She, too, is genuinely impressed.) It's beautiful.

RENE: It's the sunset.

KATIE: You're much better than me at art.

RENE: I didn't know anybody was better than you at anything.

(Awkward pause.)

RANDY: Who's interested in popcorn?

ANGELA: I'll always eat popcorn!

RANDY: Jesse, the popcorn popper's up here, right?

JESSE: I'll make it, Randy. Happy to. Like to help, Rene?

(RENE crosses to the kitchen to help.)

MAGGIE: Make sure you follow the instructions, honey.

ANGELA: I always let the oil get too hot before I put in the popcorn. You've got to time it just right. Now, check the clock, Rene.

(RENE looks at the wall clock, then at her Mother.)

RENE: Uh…

KATIE: There's a wall clock right there.

MAGGIE: Rene has her own watch. But I don't think she has it on.

RANDY, ANGELA, and CHARLIE: *(All trying to save the day.)* It's ten after eleven.

JESSE: I'll keep us on track.

(JESSE and RENE start to work in the kitchen.)

ANGELA: *(In her loud whisper.)* I'm *so* sorry. I thought she just had a problem with reading—getting her *bs* and *ds* mixed up. I didn't know she had so many problems.

MAGGIE: I focus on what Rene *can* do, not on what she can't.

RANDY: How 'bout another story, Charlie?

CHARLIE: I'm always good for a story—

ANGELA: But Maggie, is it safe for her to work in the kitchen?

MAGGIE: Rene is a good cook.

KATIE: Tell your choir initiation story, Dad.

ANGELA: I've heard *that* one.

RANDY: But you haven't heard *Maggie* tell it. She was one of the rookie choir members.

MAGGIE: I didn't think it was funny then, and I don't think it's that funny now.

(A clanging pot in the kitchen catches everyone's attention.)

MAGGIE: You OK, Rene?

JESSE: We got it covered.

RANDY: Lighten up! Tell her what happened.

MAGGIE: Well, they started by blindfolding us. All the freshmen.

ANGELA: I remember being a freshman!

MAGGIE: Then the sophomores put syrup in our hair and the juniors put molasses all over our necks.

KATIE: Ooooo!

RANDY: Isn't that great!

CHARLIE: It was sick.

MAGGIE: Then, the seniors took gold and silver glitter and poured it all over us, and it got stuck in the syrup and molasses.

KATIE: *(Giggling with delight.)* Gross!

MAGGIE: I had glitter in my hair for a week.

CHARLIE: To think that's how we "welcomed" the freshmen into the choir. Kids can be so cruel to each other.

RANDY: It was good fun.

MAGGIE: Not for me it wasn't.

(JESSE crosses out of the kitchen, with small bowls and napkins, leaving RENE alone in the kitchen.)

JESSE: Popcorn's up.

(RENE lifts the lid off of the popcorn before it is finished popping and turned off. Popcorn goes flying everywhere.)

RANDY: *(Joking.)* Hit the deck everybody.

CHARLIE: Killer popcorn!

(CHARLIE and RANDY begin throwing and dodging the popcorn. MAGGIE has raced to the kitchen, put the popcorn popper top back on and turned it off. ANGELA and KATIE are giggling at RANDY and CHARLIE's antics. JESSE has pulled back and is standing on the sidelines. MAGGIE and finally RENE herself start to laugh.)

RENE: It's snowing!

(Everyone is laughing.)

KATIE: Didn't you read the instructions?

RENE: Who reads instructions.

KATIE: I do.

RENE: I'm a popcorn "artiste!"

MAGGIE: You just got your wires crossed, honey, and did one step before the other.

KATIE: I guess that could happen to anybody.

RENE: *(To KATIE.)* Not just to somebody like me? Is that what you mean?

KATIE: I didn't mean anything. Really. I'm sorry.

RANDY: We'll help you clean it up, scout.

RENE: I do can…I can do this.

(JESSE leans down and starts to help pick up popcorn. RANDY helps too, as well as RENE and MAGGIE. An awkward pause among the group.)

CHARLIE: Anybody up for a game of cards? *(To MAGGIE.)* She can play cards, right?

MAGGIE: Of course she can.

RENE: I don't want to play. Thanks.

(Another awkward pause.)

CHARLIE: How about twister? You bring the twister, Mags? I wouldn't mind getting tangled up with somebody. *(ANGELA giggles.)*

ANGELA: Why doesn't Katie play us one of her songs!

KATIE: I couldn't.

CHARLIE: Come on, Katie. Everybody's dyin' to hear you sing.

KATIE: I can't remember any of the good ones.

CHARLIE: You haven't written a bad one.

KATIE: Well…

(ANGELA, CHARLIE, and RANDY egg her on. MAGGIE smiles encouragingly, but her focus is on RENE. JESSE is hanging back.)

KATIE: OK.

(Amidst applause, KATIE crosses to the piano.)

CHARLIE: She's gonna be top of the charts someday.

ANGELA: Shhhh!

(KATIE begins to play and sing. The music is upbeat, strangely contrary to the words.)

KATIE *(Singing.)*

"Darkness comes down now,
I can hardly see.
I feel a darkness rising in me.
Out on the outside that's where I've been.
Out on the outside, let me come in.
Look through your window, and give me some light.
Tell me you love me, say it's all right.
Open the door now, I've lost my key.
Shut out the darkness that is rising in me.
In Me. In Me. In Me. In Me."

(Applause from the group. Next three lines spoken over applause.)

CHARLIE: Bravo!

ANGELA: Isn't she wonderful?

RANDY: Terrific!

KATIE: Thank you.

CHARLIE: Bet she'll have a brand new one for us tomorrow.

RANDY: She can write something like that overnight?

KATIE: Sometimes.

RANDY: You got a gold mine here, Charlie. Started practicing your speech for the Grammies yet?

MAGGIE: It's a very pretty song. Don't you think so, Rene?

RENE: It doesn't feel like…it fits.

ANGELA: What?

RENE: I…can't explain. Doesn't matter. It's great, Katie.

JESSE: Need to be gettin' back downstairs. Thanks Randy—everybody.

RANDY: See you in the morning for breakfast.

JESSE: I—

RANDY: No arguments. I'm counting on your potatoes. Get it!

(A groan from the group for the bad joke. As JESSE exits, all say good night.)

JESSE: Night. *(He exits.)*

CHARLIE: Nice guy, Randy.

ANGELA: He's terribly quiet.

RENE: He's a poet.

ANGELA: *(Clueless.)* That must be it.

RANDY: *(Beginning to exit.)* Sunrise trail—first thing in the morning!

ANGELA, CHARLIE, MAGGIE: Oh, Randy. / Groan! / You've got to be kidding!

RANDY: Can you think of a better way to wake up?

ANGELA: Well, I don't know if I'll hike, but I do think I'm about ready for bed. Dinner was wonderful, Maggie.

MAGGIE: My pleasure.

ANGELA: Sleep tight, Katie. *(No reply from KATIE.)* Night, everybody. *(She exits.)*

CHARLIE: Well, Katie. You and Rene—sleeping in the living room! A real slumber party!

RANDY: See ya bright and early, Charlie!

CHARLIE: I don't know about that!

RANDY and CHARLIE: *(Exiting.)* Good night.

KATIE: *(Following him for a hug.)* Good night, Dad.

MAGGIE: *(To RENE.)* This OK with you?

(RENE shrugs. KATIE watches this mother/daughter scene from the doorway to the back hall.)

MAGGIE: I know I ought to be, but I'm not that sleepy. Think I'll do some stargazing on the hammock. Wanna come?

RENE: Maybe in a bit.

MAGGIE: All right, honey. Night.

(KATIE exits down the hallway to go brush her teeth. MAGGIE exits through the front door to the porch. As she opens the door, JESSE is there.)

MAGGIE: Oh.

JESSE: Sorry. Left something in the kitchen.

MAGGIE: Sure.

(JESSE crosses into the room.)

MAGGIE: Jesse, I never see all these constellations in the city. Stop by the hammock, would you? We can talk stars.

JESSE: If you want.

(MAGGIE exits. It is awkward between JESSE and RENE.)

JESSE: Your Mom. Real nice. *(RENE nods.)* Rene...the popcorn thing...I'm sorry.

RENE: It wasn't your fault.

JESSE: I said up and you went up. The lid and all.

RENE: I've done worse things. It doesn't matter.

JESSE: Yes it does. See, I you...*want* you to—

(KATIE enters. JESSE stops.)

JESSE: I'm gonna go. Good night.

(JESSE exits. KATIE and RENE are left alone in the room; RENE moves to get her sleeping bag, and starts to unroll it on the floor.)

KATIE: You can sleep on the couch. I know you weren't expecting to have to share this room.

RENE: I'd rather sleep on the floor. It's better for your back.

KATIE: What?

RENE: I learned that in movement class.

KATIE: You take dance?

RENE: Movement. It's different.

KATIE: I had to take a dance class last year. It was awful. But I had the lead in the school musical and I had to dance, so they made me take it. And then in the show, I sang *really* terribly.

RENE: Why do you say things like that?

KATIE: Like what?

RENE: You just sang great.

KATIE: I'm not as good as I should be.

RENE: And you've got to be the best?

(KATIE turns away from RENE. Silence, but then KATIE begins to laugh.)

RENE: What?

KATIE: That was so funny! Didn't you hear everybody sending you all those popcorn warnings?

RENE: No.

KATIE: Your Mom was talking right to you.

RENE: Sometimes I just…can't listen.

KATIE: Why not?

RENE: It's the way I am.

KATIE: Oh. I didn't know you had a hearing problem, too.

RENE: I don't have…forget it.

(RENE crosses to her sleeping bag.)

KATIE: I know you don't want me here. You might as well say it.

(RENE is silent.)

KATIE: You can ignore me. It's OK. I can't believe I missed a whole day of school just driving here. I'll probably fail because I missed class today.

RENE: It's real tough on you straight-A students, isn't it.

(Now it's KATIE's turn to be silent. She merely looks at RENE. RENE gets up and crosses to the lamp to turn it off.)

KATIE: *(Turning over to go to sleep.)* I'll probably fail.

(RENE turns off the light. She is left in the glow of the moonlight. She sits down to paint. Lights isolate her as she begins to voice her thoughts.)

RENE: Map it. Map her away. Take the line for a walk around the page. Make it strong. Curved. Turn sharp. Go under. Over. Just get around her. Paint her as a hurdle. Jump! Red. She's red. Cadmium. Staining. More water. *(She adds more water to her brush.)* Get weaker! Fade! Please fade! Let the white show through. See through it. To the paper. To the white. *(RENE is now being bombarded by school memories. We hear KATIE's voice, laughing.)* New line. Cut the page in half. Make room—for you! A room…

KATIE'S VOICE: That's the room for "study skills."

RENE: Not silent.

KATIE'S VOICE: Ever hear them?

RENE: All voices *your* voice.

KATIE'S VOICE: S-o-u-n-d-i-n-g out the w-o-r-d-s!

RENE: Stop. Please.

KATIE'S VOICE: Sounds like they're from another planet.

RENE: Make room. What color? For you! Bright. Yellow. Cadmium Yellow… Pale. No, red stains yellow. Covers it. Blue. Cobalt. No! Ocean! You could sink! Make a color. Mix it. Use them. Use them all. *(The result.)* Mud—gray—brown. Nothing! Nothing!

(LIGHTS return to realism, and we realize that RENE is now calling out loud and throwing her paint brushes and painting books from the desk onto the floor. MAGGIE hears her, and runs quickly from the porch. She is followed by JESSE.)

RENE: Nothing! Mud-gray-brown!

MAGGIE: Rene.

RENE: Mud! Brown!

(KATIE wakes up from the commotion, but she stays on the couch, watching.)

MAGGIE: *(Trying to hold RENE.)* Stop it!

RENE: Gray! Nothing. Fading…

MAGGIE: What is it? Honey, tell me.

RENE: *(Crying.)* My pictures. I find…can't *find* them.

MAGGIE: What?

RENE: You don't stand…understand!

MAGGIE: I want to—more than anything.

KATIE: What's wrong? What happened?

(RENE, remembering KATIE's presence, is humiliated. She wrenches away from her mother, and runs toward the door, but she sees JESSE.)

JESSE: Rene—

(Doubly humiliated, RENE rushes over to the desk, and clutches her paints. She sits and strokes the paper with her hand.)

KATIE: What's wrong with her?

JESSE: *(Crossing to Katie, quietly.)* Shhhhh.

MAGGIE: You want to paint, sweetheart, for a little while?

(RENE shakes her head, but continues to stroke the paper.)

MAGGIE: I'll be right here.

JESSE: Try to sleep, Katie.

MAGGIE: I'm right here, honey. Right here.

(JESSE looks at RENE, then exits quietly, closing the door behind him.)
(LIGHTS OUT. Music transition.)

SCENE FOUR

LIGHTS UP on early Saturday morning. RENE is by the window, painting. She appears brighter, calmer. Occasionally, she opens a piece of paper, and studies it. KATIE is sitting on the couch, but still snuggled down in her sleeping bag. CHARLIE and MAGGIE are gathered around the coffeemaker, like a shrine, waiting for a cup. RANDY bursts through the door in full hiking attire.

RANDY: You missed it!

MAGGIE: Save it, Randy.

RANDY: How could you guys possibly stay in bed on a morning like this?

CHARLIE: We managed.

(ANGELA emerges from the bedroom hallway, dressed in the latest Banana Republic outdoor wear.)

ANGELA: Good morning.

RANDY: I'll say.

ANGELA: *(Referring to her attire.)* You like it? I thought it was just right for a day in the mountains. Come on, Katie, up and at 'em.

KATIE: Nooo.

RANDY: Did you two stay up and talk all night?

CHARLIE: You slept in your clothes! What'd you do that for?

ANGELA: *(Winking.)* Modesty.

(RANDY gestures to CHARLIE. They exchange a knowing look, then sneak up on KATIE.)

RANDY: *(Cartoon voice.)* What she needs is—

RANDY and CHARLIE: The ole high school rise and shine!

(They grab the top of KATIE's sleeping bag and carry her, kicking and screaming, and laughing, through the door to the bedrooms.)

CHARLIE: Special delivery!

RANDY: To your private dressing room, Madame.

KATIE: You guys!!

(They exit with KATIE, laughing.)

MAGGIE: Want some coffee?

ANGELA: Love some. How do you do it, Maggie?

MAGGIE: Coffee?

ANGELA: No! I mean, well, it's been six months since Charlie's divorce was final. And, Katie, well, it's obvious, isn't it?

MAGGIE: I'm a beat behind, Angela.

ANGELA: *(Laughs uncomfortably.)* Oh, Charlie says I have the biggest mouth in southern California. But when it comes to anything important, I—is there a formula—magic words or something—that can turn me into a Mom?

(RANDY and CHARLIE come laughing back into the room.)

CHARLIE: Teenagers!

ANGELA: *(Her old self.)* You guys, or Katie?

RANDY: We're just clownin' around. Katie needs to lighten up.

CHARLIE: Oh?

RANDY: Ease up on herself. Get a life outside the books. *(To MAGGIE.)* What do you think, "Mom?"

MAGGIE: *(Looking at ANGELA.)* I don't have all the answers. I wish I did.

RANDY: She needs a boyfriend.

CHARLIE: Watch it.

ANGELA: Leave her to me! We'll get her a new haircut. Maybe an exercise class.

CHARLIE: She's gotta stop knockin' herself. She's got everything goin' for her.

ANGELA: She just needs a little attention.

CHARLIE: I am constantly praising her—telling her she's fantastic. What else do you want me to do?

(ANGELA cannot reply.)

CHARLIE: Hey Rene, let us know if you figure Katie out.

RENE: OK.

(JESSE enters through the front door, half-way knocking as he comes.)

JESSE: Mornin'.

MAGGIE: It's the chef.

(Everybody wishes him good morning; RENE looks at him, with a kind of embarrassed smile.)

JESSE: Breakfast is up—*(Correcting himself.)* ready.

RANDY: All right! Home fries, scrambled eggs—

(All but RENE start moving toward the door, eager for breakfast.)

CHARLIE: I haven't had a breakfast like this since our Pep club overnights.

RANDY: Oh, man! We'd start with a hayride—

MAGGIE: *(To RANDY.)* Tell us about them at breakfast, OK?

RANDY: I'm getting in touch with my inner teenager—

MAGGIE: Eat!

(RANDY, ANGELA, and CHARLIE pile out the door.)

JESSE: Like griddle cakes, Rene?

RENE: Sure. In a minute.

MAGGIE: *(To JESSE.)* We'll be down.

(JESSE leaves, closing the door with a look to RENE and MAGGIE.)

MAGGIE: You hungry? Need a good breakfast to do the waterfall hike.

RENE: *(Unfolding the piece of paper.)* Mom, will you read this to me?

MAGGIE: I'll help *you* read it. What is it?

RENE: It's a poem. Jesse's poem. He gave it to me yesterday.

MAGGIE: On your walk? *(RENE nods.)* Try out loud.

RENE: Mom—

MAGGIE: Try.

RENE: *(Reading.)* "Soft gray blue light, Re-ve…

MAGGIE: Sound it out.

RENE: "Re-ve…" *(Hands her the paper.)* You read it. Please?

MAGGIE: *(Reading.)* "Soft gray-blue light. Reveals the perfection of the morning."

(MAGGIE pauses as she looks at the page, noticing the handwriting and spelling.)

RENE: Go on.

MAGGIE: "I awake to the wonder
of my aloneness.
I have an eternity,
A whole day before me."

RENE: That's pretty. He finds words—good ones.

MAGGIE: So can you, honey.

RENE: *(Getting up and going to the desk.)* This morning, I painted something. See the yellow? That's the sun. Rising. It colors everything, see? And sparkles. *(Crossing to the window.)* See the dew? It shimmers.

MAGGIE: *(Giving her a big hug.)* Here's my girl. Here you are. Don't disappear again, please?

RENE: I'm yellow. I've decided.

MAGGIE: *(Laughing.)* You're bouncin' back like a Superball.

RENE: Now go eat.

MAGGIE: Come with me.

RENE: I gotta do something. Go ahead.

MAGGIE: Mystery woman! All right, sunshine. Love you bunches.

RENE: Double bunches.

(MAGGIE exits. RENE crosses to the desk, and picks up a piece of paper and a pencil. She crosses to the couch and lies down on the floor in front of the couch. RENE is struggling to compose words in her head, a poem. She silently muses, and then carefully, slowly writes the words on the painting.)

KATIE, quietly, sticks her head in around the corner from the bedrooms.
She has a notebook in her hand. She looks around the room. She cannot see
Rene on the floor. [She is blocked by the couch.]
    KATIE crosses over toward the desk and begins to quickly look across the
spines of all the books, searching.
    KATIE does not immediately find what she wants. Then she turns and
sees a book of poems. She flips through the pages to find one she wants. She
opens her notebook, and begins to copy a poem from the book. She is just near-
ing the end when RENE gives a satisfied sigh upon completion of her poem.
    The sigh startles KATIE, who slams the book shut with a start. The noise
startles RENE, who gasps.)
KATIE: Ah!
RENE: *Ah!!*
KATIE: What are you doing here?
RENE: Writing.
KATIE: Have you been watching me? Following me?
RENE: I didn't see you come in. I was concentrating.
    (KATIE is uneasy, agitated.)
RENE: Look. I'm walking down to breakfast. You want to come?
KATIE: I'm…not ready yet.
RENE: I'll wait.
KATIE: You don't have to. I'd rather you didn't.
RENE: Fine. *(RENE picks up her jacket and crosses toward the door, then turns*
    back.) Katie—
KATIE: Would you go!
    (RENE crosses back to make sure her poem is put away. KATIE is now des-
    perate to get rid of her.)
KATIE: You better hurry. Your Mom might steal your new boyfriend.
RENE: What are you talking about?
KATIE: "Wanna talk stars?" On the *hammock!* If he were mine, I wouldn't let
    anybody get in the way.
RENE: You're crazy. Nobody's anybody's boyfriend.
KATIE: Maybe your Mom'll go for my Dad, too. They dated in high school,
    you know.
RENE: Katie, what's this about? Just cause you don't like your Dad with
    Angela—
KATIE: I haven't said I don't like it.
RENE: You don't have to. It shows.
KATIE: You're a mind reader?

RENE: I can tell things about people.

KATIE: Rene, do you want to be friends?

(RENE gives a noncommittal shrug.)

KATIE: Then would you start by doing what I ask and leave me *alone!* Get out! Please.

(RENE starts to go, but comes back into the room.)

RENE: What *is* it with you this morning?

KATIE: *(Hiding the notebook.)* What do you mean?

RENE: I can look at you, and see something wrong. Why are you hiding your notebook?

KATIE: I'm not! So, you see something wrong, do you—with *me?* What do you think people see when they look at you?

RENE: Me.

KATIE: *(Grabbing RENE's poem from her.)* Dad said they could tell from the day you were born that you were "special"—"different"—why don't they just say it—"slow!"

RENE: Why are you...I'm not—

KATIE: Maybe that's why it's just you—you and your Mom. Just the two of you. Nobody else!

(RENE grabs the poem back from KATIE and clutches it.)

KATIE: Cause nobody else wants to get near someone so special—so especially screwed up!

RENE: *(Trying to speak but her sequence gets all mixed up.)* Mom my...true not...Jess...yellow...stop!

KATIE: What language is that, Rene? Now get out. *Get out!*

(RENE runs from the cabin. KATIE pauses a moment, then rushes back to the desk, and quickly finishes copying the poem. She closes her notebook. LIGHTS OUT. Music transition.)

SCENE FIVE

LIGHTS UP on the "Looking Spot." RENE is seated hugging her knees, her face still wet with tears. She looks out across the view. JESSE enters. He sees her, stops for a moment, then crosses up to her.

JESSE: What do you see? *(No reply.)* This is the looking spot. Can't come up here if you're not gonna look. *(He sits next to her.)* Leaves are just startin' to change. See those trees over there? All yellow and red.

(RENE shrinks further at the reference to yellow and red.)

JESSE: Don't like yellow and red? How 'bout some orange. Golden orange. Pick something out to see. Make you feel better.

(RENE still does not reply.)

JESSE: The clouds are nice—real lacy. What'd you think?

RENE: Pretty lacy.

JESSE: Lots of little threads. It's fragile, up there. Bet it'll be all pink when the day grows up.

RENE: Jesse, what's it like—the day you grow up?

JESSE: What?

RENE: When you grow up, do you get to stop who...*being* who you are and be somebody else?

JESSE: You think there's a magic day when you get to trade one Rene in for another?

RENE: I hope so. I don't want this Rene anymore. *(She picks up a small rock.)* I wish I could toss the right-now-stupid-me right over the—

JESSE: Hey, not so close! Let's just keep sittin', OK?

(RENE curls back up, shut off.)

JESSE: Have you ever seen the rings on the inside of a tree?

RENE: Yeah.

JESSE: You know how it gets those rings? *(RENE shrugs.)* See, a tree starts out being pretty little, but as it grows up, it keeps addin' rings of age—circles of life.

RENE: So?

JESSE: No matter how big a tree gets, it's still got the little tree inside it, right in the middle. You oughta try to start likin' the Rene you are right now, cause she's always gonna be there, right in the middle.

RENE: Have you still got a little-kid Jesse in the middle of you?

JESSE: There's a real grumpy little guy, about eight years old, who takes a swing at anyone who looks at him sideways. And there's a freshman in high school, who sits in a classroom, lookin' out the window. But not seein' out. He always gets stuck, lookin' at his own reflection in the glass. He can't see past it.

RENE: Bet your school wasn't like mine is. Everyone in high school is one giant Katie—perfect grade machines who cut you into pieces so small that nothing...there's nothing left.

JESSE: You think that's all Katie is?

RENE: I'm not gonna let her or anybody get to me. Ever. I'm gonna be so strong. So *red!*

JESSE: Ah. Build a big wall—

RENE: Paint it!

JESSE: Paint a big wall around you, and never let anybody knock it down.

RENE: Exactly.

JESSE: That's what I did in high school.

RENE: See. It works.

JESSE: It's real safe inside there.

RENE: Nobody can hurt you.

JESSE: Hurt yourself mostly.

RENE: What?

JESSE: You can't feel much behind a wall. If you can't feel, how're you ever gonna understand? About yourself or about anybody else?

(RENE shrugs.)

JESSE: How you ever gonna figure out what's wrong with Katie?

RENE: Katie's perfect, remember!

JESSE: You think so? You've got...you're blessed with so many things. Don't lock yourself up, cause one part of you makes life a little hard.

RENE: How can *you* know how hard it is? Have you ever had one thought in your brain and had another one come out of your mouth? Have you ever booked...*looked* in a book and seen the words fall off the edge of the page? Or wake up one morning and you think, "I thought the world was out of whack. But it's not! It's me! It's *me!*"

JESSE: I...*(He stops.)*

RENE: Why should I try to understand anybody else when nobody can understand me!

(JESSE is silent.)

RENE: I don't want to "look" anymore. Look by yourself.

(RENE exits. JESSE looks after her but does not follow.)

(LIGHTS OUT. Music Transition.)

SCENE SIX

LIGHTS UP on RENE at her water color table. All other characters are in their places on stage, but they are frozen and in darkness. She is again voicing her thoughts as she paints.

RENE: On the cave wall. Rough. The edges are sharp. Like teeth. She paints— a boundary. A barricade. Lines "x-ing" a pattern. "Xs." Mark it. This is the spot. Ringed by fire. The center of all maps. You others, outside, you're afraid of fire, aren't you? Purple-red, gold—a ring burning.

(A light comes up on KATIE, still frozen.)

RENE: Dare you. Take a step. See? You run! Back run. Down the page. You— disappear? Ooze and smear, no edges, no shape—so why still red?!

(A light comes up on JESSE, frozen, in the kitchen.)

RENE: No. Watch out! You'll get burned!

(She repositions her brush.)

RENE: Stay there. Near the edge. Pretty. Cool, blue—distant. Don't mix with the others. Please. Look out—the other way.

(Lights up on CHARLIE, RANDY, MAGGIE, and ANGELA, frozen, set for card playing at a table.)

RENE: See me? I'm here. In the middle. Follow the map. To the Xs. Can you step around the fire, Mom?

(Turning toward her Mom, then turning away.)

RENE: Please, stay—on other side. *(To everyone.)* Can you always see me? In the middle of circles? Of rings? Rings of *fire!* No one touches. I am bright. Hot! Bright…

(Full lights up to realism inside the cabin, right before dinner on Saturday. RANDY, CHARLIE, ANGELA, and MAGGIE are all playing cards. JESSE is in the kitchen, working on dinner. KATIE is at the piano, working on her song. RENE crosses to the card game, seemingly full of spunk and confidence, and cheers on her Mom.)

CHARLIE: One, two, three, *spit!*

(All players slap a card onto the table, and a raucous game sequence begins in which each player tries to build either up or down on the card that has been laid down. The following lines are overlapping and rapid.)

ANGELA: Four, five, six—

RANDY: *I* had a six! Ah! Jack, Queen, King.

MAGGIE: Ouch!

RENE: Uncle Randy!

MAGGIE: You hit me. *(Slapping down cards.)* Ah, ten, nine, ten—

CHARLIE: God, you're quick!

RENE: Go, Mom!

ANGELA: Three, two, three, four!

RANDY: Five, six, five, four, five! Love it! Love it!

ANGELA: Was he always this good?

RANDY: A champ!

MAGGIE: A cheat.

RANDY: Who cheats? Charlie cheats!

CHARLIE: How did I cheat? I put down a five, six, seven...nine!

ALL PLAYERS: Ah *ha!!!* Cheat!

CHARLIE: It wasn't intentional!

MAGGIE: Sure, Charlie!

RENE: I bet.

ANGELA: I better watch you, if you're a cheater.

> *(CHARLIE begins to get the cards back into piles.)*

MAGGIE: Jesse, we missed you on the waterfall hike.

CHARLIE/ANGELA: Yeah, we missed you. Where were you?

RANDY: You should've seen Rene. Bounding ahead of everybody.

MAGGIE: I didn't know she could move that fast.

RANDY: Who were you racin' against?

RENE: I won, didn't I? You missed it, Jesse!

JESSE: I had to look...take my own walk.

RANDY: You OK?

JESSE: Fine.

ANGELA: *(Giving CHARLIE a kiss.)* I thought it was incredibly romantic.

RANDY: *(To JESSE.)* Wanna join in the game?

JESSE: Doin' dinner.

RENE: I don't think Jesse likes games.

CHARLIE: I'm just glad you're cookin' tonight. I thought we were stuck with Mags.

ANGELA: You girls enjoyed the waterfall, didn't you?

RENE: It was real "special." Wasn't it, Katie.

> *(KATIE receives RENE's cut, and does not reply.)*

RANDY: Well! We'll just hike back tomorrow, no problem.

CHARLIE: *(Amidst groans of others.)* What, are you crazy?

ANGELA: Come on, back to the game! I was winning!

CHARLIE: You want to play, Katie?

> *(KATIE moves to join the circle.)*

ANGELA: Not in the middle of a game!

> *(KATIE moves away.)*

MAGGIE: *(To KATIE.)* You can take my place.

ANGELA: *(Trying to makeup.)* Or mine.

KATIE: I've got to finish this—my song—anyway.

> *(KATIE crosses back to the piano.)*

ANGELA: Then, come on, *spit* everybody!

(CHARLIE and RANDY have a great time with the command, dramatically preparing to spit.)
ANGELA: Spit the cards, gentlemen, the cards!
RANDY: Spoilsport.
CHARLIE: OK. One, two, three, *spit!*
RENE: Go Mom.
ANGELA: *(Amid the quick playing of card and grumbles and cheers of the others.)* Three, four, five, *out!!* I won!
MAGGIE: I *still* can't win this game.
RANDY: One more round.
CHARLIE: Let's give the girls a turn. Here you are, ladies. Face off.
(The girls stare at one another. Neither moves.)
ANGELA: What? Have you girls got some secret or something?
KATIE: Of course not.
RENE: You guys go ahead.
ANGELA: How 'bout crazy eights?
MAGGIE: So now we're progressing to *sixth* grade?!
CHARLIE: Gin rummy, then.
RANDY: You're gettin' serious, Charlie.
MAGGIE: Don't get too serious. Looks like dinner's almost up.
JESSE: Fifteen minutes.
MAGGIE: Katie, you want to help—
RENE: *(Moving toward the kitchen.)* I'll help you.
JESSE: Don't know that I need it.
(RENE stops. She looks at JESSE.)
JESSE: *(To the Group.)* How hard are sloppy joes?
RANDY: Cafeteria food! Perfect!
MAGGIE and CHARLIE: Randy!!!
(They playfully toss a few cards at RANDY. RENE crosses away from the kitchen, to a place in the room, away from the others.)
ANGELA: *(Stands.)* Well! While you guys clown around, I'm going to dress for dinner.
CHARLIE: This is a cabin in the woods, Angela. You don't dress for dinner.
ANGELA: I do. *(She exits.)*
RANDY: Go for a fast hand?
CHARLIE: I'm with ya.
(RANDY deals the cards, and CHARLIE and RANDY have a concentrated game of Gin. JESSE crosses out of the kitchen to check the wood in the stove. MAGGIE crosses to him.)

MAGGIE: The fire's nice, Jesse.

JESSE: Just tryin' to keep it warm for you folks.

MAGGIE: Don't you get cold?

JESSE: No.

MAGGIE: Do you get much snow up here?

JESSE: Some.

MAGGIE: Bad enough for chains? On your tires?

JESSE: Maggie, what do you want to say?

MAGGIE: I need to know your gift. With Rene.

JESSE: Wouldn't say I have one.

MAGGIE: You've worked *some* kind of magic on her. She's on top of the world. Don't you think?

(JESSE does not reply.)

MAGGIE: I try to get inside her shoes, know what she feels—

JESSE: You can't.

MAGGIE: I can try.

JESSE: But you'll never *know*.

(A big burst of laughter from the card table.)

RANDY: Shmuck!

CHARLIE: Champ!

(RENE crosses and sees her Mom and JESSE talking. She tries to clear past them, going back down the hallway to the bedrooms.)

MAGGIE: Sunshine, help me finish up in the kitchen.

JESSE: I could use some more wood, here, too.

(RENE does not cross to either, unsure of what's up.)

MAGGIE: Come on over when you're done.

(MAGGIE crosses to the kitchen. RENE stays with JESSE, but keeps her distance.)

JESSE: Get a bunch.

(RENE picks up one small piece of wood. They cross to the stove.)

JESSE: You really like the waterfall?

RENE: It was smaller than I thought it would be.

JESSE: Know why that is?

RENE: I'm sure you'll tell me.

JESSE: It's not real. They made it, reroutin' the water through here.

RENE: Interesting.

JESSE: Pile it in good. Need a big fire.

RENE: *(Thinking of her own images.)* But don't…get burned.

JESSE: I won't. The poem I gave you. You never said.

RENE: Said what?

JESSE: If you liked it.

RENE: Kinda.

JESSE: Ah. Guess somebody behind a big wall can only kinda like a poem.

(RENE crosses quickly away from JESSE, heading back to her paints. Her false front is starting to slip.)

CHARLIE: Gin! *Ha!*

(KATIE plays a line on the piano.)

RANDY: Hey Beethoven, is that your new song?

KATIE: Yes—

CHARLIE: What'd I tell you.

RANDY: Let's hear it. Doesn't everybody want to hear it?

KATIE: Not yet! This song has to be perfect. It's for my honors class.

RANDY: Perfect. Smerfect—

CHARLIE: *(Cutting him off.)* Randy! *(To KATIE.)* Play it, sweetheart.

KATIE: I've worked forever on it. I don't know if the words are good enough—

CHARLIE: Play it. Listen everybody.

(KATIE sits and begins to play and sing.)

KATIE: *(Singing.)*
"Who has seen the wind.
Neither I nor you.
But when the leaves hang trembling,
The wind is passing through."

(ANGELA enters in a new outfit. She slips quietly in to listen, smiling.)
"Who has seen the wind.
Neither you nor I.
But when the leaves bow down their heads,
The wind is passing by."

(Applause. KATIE stands to bow amid congratulations.)

ANGELA: Oh, I loved that poem in high school. It makes a beautiful song.

(KATIE is silent. Everyone shifts awkwardly.)

ANGELA: Well it does! Don't you guys remember it? Who wrote it? Christina Rossetti. That's who.

CHARLIE: Katie, is she right?

(KATIE looks at ANGELA.)

CHARLIE: Is Angela right?!

KATIE: She...She's—

CHARLIE: You said you wrote the words yourself!

KATIE: I...

CHARLIE: Answer me!

ANGELA: Oh, Charlie, it's OK—

CHARLIE: My daughter is not going to lie to me or to any one else. Katie, why did you—

KATIE: I'm…sorry…

(*KATIE throws the music on the floor and bursts out of the cabin.*)

CHARLIE: (*Trying to laugh.*) Well. Sorry everybody.

ANGELA: Shouldn't we go after her?

CHARLIE: Let her calm down first. I hate talkin' to her when she's crying.

RANDY: Ahh, tears make Dad a marshmallow, huh?

CHARLIE: Lay off, Randy!

RANDY: It was a *joke.*

MAGGIE: Somebody should try. Angela—

CHARLIE: She can't. (*ANGELA shrinks.*)

JESSE: Rene could.

RENE: Me?

JESSE: Least she could have yesterday. Don't know about now.

CHARLIE: Why not? *I* sure don't get what's goin' on.

JESSE: (*To RENE.*) See if she wants to talk.

RENE: Why?

JESSE: Oh, that's right. You don't wanna know—find out anything anymore.

MAGGIE: What?

RENE: (*To JESSE.*) You don't think find…*I* can find out why a person hurts?

(*RENE accepts JESSE's challenge. She crosses toward the door. She picks up her jacket right before her mother tells her to.*)

MAGGIE: Honey, be careful. Take a…jacket.

(*RENE exits. The door slams.*)

ANGELA: What do we do, Maggie?

MAGGIE: We wait. We let go. And we wait.

(*ANGELA takes a step toward CHARLIE, then rushes back to her bedroom. MAGGIE sits by herself. RANDY crosses to JESSE. LIGHTS OUT. Music transition.*)

SCENE SEVEN

LIGHTS UP on the Looking Spot. RENE is climbing up on to the rock. KATIE is lagging behind.

RENE: Did you feel it? It gets cooler. Lighter.

KATIE: No.

RENE: You've got to look. Did you smell the eucalyptus? It was real strong.
(KATIE is silent.)

RENE: Now look out. Pick something.

KATIE: Why?

RENE: See that tree? It's not the same as the others. It's bluer—the needles—pricklier. Or the stream. See it? It sings.

KATIE: I was just caught lying in front of all those people and you want me to look at the trees?

RENE: It'll help.

KATIE: I don't want your help.

RENE: Then why'd you come with me?
(KATIE looks at RENE. Finally she sits down on the rocks.)

RENE: Over there, there's a town. The roads, look like strings.

KATIE: I wish I could stop shaking.

RENE: *(Straight-shot.)* Then tell me what's wrong.

KATIE: You were there! You saw.

RENE: Why'd you do it?

KATIE: I had to. How else can I be the best?

RENE: Can't you words...write your own words?

KATIE: What are they? Now my Dad knows I'm a liar. Knows I'm a fake.

RENE: So talk to him.

KATIE: No.

RENE: He's your Dad.

KATIE: So? You can't understand. What it's like. I don't know how to be any-thing...but everybody has to think I'm...the best...and now no one...

RENE: Katie. Stop shaking. What can you see? Please.

KATIE: Nothing. Falling. Floating. I...
(KATIE takes a step toward the edge of the rocks.)

RENE: Katie, what are...*stop it!*

KATIE: I hate her!

RENE: Who?

KATIE: Katie.

RENE: What? *Why?* You're talented, you're straight-As, you're—
KATIE: That's *why!* I hate it if I win and I hate it when I don't. It's a contest. Always. With myself.
RENE: Katie, I'm in a contest with *life* everyday. I can't read a clock. I get lost in my own house! There's always something me...to trip me. Something I can't do! But I just *do.*
KATIE: I don't know how.
RENE: *(PAUSE.)* You've never failed? At anything? Ever?
(KATIE shakes her head.)
RENE: I wish I had your problem.
KATIE: I wish I had yours.
RENE: Are you scared of school?
KATIE: Yeah.
RENE: Just like me?
(KATIE nods. KATIE and RENE sit quietly. RENE looks out across the mountains.)
RENE: Look. It's the light from the lighthouse. Way out! See it? You don't see that very often. What do you see?
KATIE: *(Looking out for the first time.)* Clouds.
RENE: What else?
KATIE: Colors.
RENE: Where?
KATIE: There. There's yellow—on a rock. I've never seen that before.
(The girls smile and look out across the mountains.)
(LIGHTS OUT. Music transition.)

SCENE EIGHT

LIGHTS UP on the cabin, mid-morning on Sunday. CHARLIE is cleaning mud off of his boots. ANGELA is zipping up a garment bag. RANDY is seated at the table with his map spread. MAGGIE is in the kitchen.

RANDY: *(Checking his digital watch.)* Sunday. 10:32 AM. Only 12.7 miles. I've become a hiking wimp.
CHARLIE: Randy, for God's sake. You hiked circles around the rest of us.
ANGELA: *(Struggling to zip her bag.)* Maybe if you had jogged, Randy, you might have covered more ground.

RANDY: Jogged! By God, I could've jogged some of those trails. Come on Charlie, one for the road.

ANGELA: *(Unhappy at the idea.)* Charlie…

MAGGIE: I don't think he's going anywhere.

(KATIE enters through the door from the porch. She is carrying a bunch of wildflowers. RENE follows her and crosses to her Uncle.)

ANGELA: Katie!

MAGGIE: *(To Girls.)* Have a good walk?

(The girls nod. It is clear they have an agenda.)

CHARLIE: Ready to hit the road, Katie? Long drive back to San Diego.

KATIE: Almost.

CHARLIE: You got cruise-control on your car, Randy?

RANDY: Not me. Nothing but a stick shift for me. See, I—

RENE: *(Cutting him off.)* Uncle Randy, can I show you something outside?

RANDY: Outside?

RENE: Uh-huh.

RANDY: *(Getting it.)* Sure. Why not. Get the dishes later, Mags.

(RANDY exits out the front door.)

RENE: Mom…

MAGGIE: Right! I should get my things packed.

(MAGGIE heads back to the bedroom. KATIE looks to RENE, a little desperate, but RENE smiles, closing the front door behind her.)

CHARLIE: *(Uncomfortable.)* Still trying to get the mud off my boots from yesterday.

KATIE: Dad—

CHARLIE: Muddy going down to that water fall. Sure was pretty though.

ANGELA: Charlie!

CHARLIE: Didn't you think so, Angela?

ANGELA: Katie's…here.

KATIE: All right. So shoot.

ANGELA: *(Turning to leave.)* I'll…wait out here—

KATIE: No. Stay. If you want. *(ANGELA stays.)* I took a walk this morning. A long walk. Trying to find something.

CHARLIE: Did you lose something? What—where'd you lose it?

KATIE: *(Close to tears.)* You're not listening.

CHARLIE: I'm listening! I'm all ears!

ANGELA: Are you?

KATIE: I looked and I looked and I couldn't find her.

CHARLIE: Who, honey?

KATIE: The Katie I made. Out of grades and honors and clapping and fear and failures I could never tell you about and—

CHARLIE: Slow down.

KATIE: And I was so happy, 'cause I thought she was gone. I want her to be. But she's strong.

CHARLIE: Look, about this poem thing—

KATIE: *(Upset.)* Dad!!

CHARLIE: *What?!*

ANGELA: Katie, you're saying…what you mean…it's bigger, isn't it.

KATIE: It's so scary.

CHARLIE: What are you scared of?

KATIE: Losing.

CHARLIE: Losing what?

KATIE: 'Cause I was thinking, on my walk, if I lose her, *(To CHARLIE.)* will I lose you?

CHARLIE: Oh, honey. You're…you're stuck with me. Don't know how much good I am, but…

ANGELA: But what?

CHARLIE: But I don't want you…or me…to push so hard, that we're goin' nowhere.

(CHARLIE pauses. ANGELA and KATIE are still listening.)

CHARLIE: I wanna see *you.*

(KATIE nods and smiles. She hands the wildflowers, which have been twisted to pieces by KATIE's nervousness, to ANGELA.)

KATIE: You can have these…

(The mangled flowers break the tension between KATIE and ANGELA. They laugh. ANGELA tentatively touches KATIE. For the first time, KATIE does not recoil. For CHARLIE, it's not so easy.)

CHARLIE: OK.

ANGELA: Well.

(It is awkward among them, but there is promise.)

CHARLIE: Hey Mags, we're outta here.

(MAGGIE enters from the back hallway, with suitcases.)

ANGELA: Thank you for everything, Maggie.

MAGGIE: I'm glad you came.

(RENE comes back in the cabin. She and KATIE exchange a look, letting RENE know that KATIE survived.)

CHARLIE: Let's not let another millennium go by before we do this again!

MAGGIE: You're the one who never calls.

ANGELA: Wait! Emergency. Left my Frescas in the fridge.

KATIE: I need a Coke, too. Want one, Rene?

RENE: Sure.

ANGELA: *(To KATIE.)* Is the cooler in the car?

(ANGELA and KATIE cross into the kitchen. CHARLIE and MAGGIE share a quick good-bye.)

MAGGIE: You gonna make it, "Dad?"

CHARLIE: When I hear that? Sometimes, I still don't realize she's talking to me.

ANGELA: *(Crossing out of the kitchen.)* Three for the road! Have you got everything, Katie?

KATIE: *(Picking up her backpack. Everyone is moving toward the door.)* I think so.

CHARLIE: *(Exiting.)* You can always come stay with us. There's loads of room.

ANGELA: *(Exiting.)* And the beach. Heaven! Nine months out of the year.

MAGGIE: *(Exiting.)* Better pack up your paints, Rene.

(RENE crosses to her painting table. KATIE, who had lagged behind the rest, turns back to RENE.)

KATIE: Is there one that, if you don't mind, I could take with me? One with a view, if you've got one.

RENE: *(Handing her a painting.)* Lots of yellow in this one. I'm glad you want it.

KATIE: You can write me some time, if you want. Or paint to me. Whatever you want. *(RENE nods.)* Bye, Rene. Thanks.

RENE: Bye.

(KATIE leaves. RENE is left alone, content. She begins to put her tubes of paint back into her box. The LIGHTS change. She begins to voice her thoughts.)

RENE: Ultramarine blue. Alizarin Crimson. *(Picking up her brushes.)* Number 12. Number 8. *(Picking up her other materials.)* A pencil. An eraser. And water. My tools. My picks and scrapers. Hammers and flint. To dig deeper. Making forever marks on the walls of the days in the redwoods. Most artists start by painting what they *know*. You have to *learn* how to paint what you *see*. *(Picking up her pad.)* A whole pad of pages. Bright and blank. Shining. Waiting. Ready.

(JESSE enters. RENE turns and the LIGHTS return to realism.)

JESSE: Shouldn't you be outside? Everybody's packin' up.

RENE: I've been looking for you.

JESSE: Didn't want to be in the way.

RENE: You look funny.

JESSE: Slept outside. I waited up. Needed to make sure somebody got back all right.

RENE: *(She hands him a piece of paper with a poem.)* Here. It's for you. I wrote it. A poem. First one. Read it.

(JESSE starts to read it silently.)

RENE: No, out loud.

(JESSE pauses.)

RENE: Please, Jesse. I haven't heard it out loud, the way poems are supposed to be.

JESSE: I can't.

RENE: *(Still urging him.)* Jesse!

JESSE: I read…

(Slowly, correcting himself.)

JESSE: I can't read out loud.

RENE: What?

JESSE: Couldn't read at all for a long time. Every time I tried, all the words on the page ended up looking like alphabet soup, you know? My teachers, they thought I was lazy. So I pretended nothing was wrong. I still do.

RENE: Ever had trouble with hopscotch?

JESSE: *(Laughs.)* No. But I scored two points for the other team in a basketball game once. *(They laugh.)* Not easy, is it.

RENE: *(Taking the poem from JESSE.)* I'll sound it out.

"I am colors bright

See the new light?

Flashing, beaming across the night?"

JESSE: That's it?

RENE: Yeah. I'm a beginner!

JESSE: *(Smiling.)* No you're not.

RENE: You can already read to yourself. Reading out loud is the step…next step.

(JESSE shakes his head.)

RENE: You scared?

JESSE: Yeah!

RENE: Next time I come, please read to me.

(MAGGIE enters through the cabin's front door.)

MAGGIE: Oh. Sorry. It's time to go, Rene. You ready?

RENE: *(To JESSE.)* Not until I know if there's gonna be a next time.

JESSE: *(To RENE.)* Give me three weeks.

RENE: You're on.

(RANDY bursts through the door, obviously having just jogged a trail.)

RANDY: Tremendous! Fifteen minutes and twenty-nine seconds straight up, then straight down.

MAGGIE: Oh my God.

RANDY: I *love* these mountains.

RENE: So do I.

RANDY: So when you comin' back, scout?

RENE: Three weeks.

MAGGIE: She's already decided—

RANDY: Deal, if Jesse'll put up with us.

(JESSE smiles and nods.)

RANDY: We're on! *(To RENE.)* Race you to the car?

RENE: *(Teasing him.)* Well, if you think you're up to it.

RANDY: Rene, you underestimate me! I can do anything.

RENE: So can I. *Go!*

(RENE holds the door open for RANDY to go racing through, while she very calmly starts to leave.)

RANDY *(From offstage.)* Hey Rene. Rene!??

RENE: Teenagers!

(She smiles and exits. MAGGIE and JESSE laugh. Then MAGGIE turns back to JESSE, she sees the poem that RENE has given him.)

JESSE: Maybe you should have this.

(MAGGIE reads the poem.)

MAGGIE: That's a blessing. It's yours. Bye.

(MAGGIE exits. JESSE is alone in the cabin. He picks up RENE's painting with the poem.)

JESSE: *(Beginning to read out loud, slowly.)* "I am co-lors br-ight. S-see the new l-light…" Three weeks.

END OF PLAY

Mary Hall Surface is an internationally-acclaimed playwright, director and producer of theatre for young audiences and families. Her work has been presented at the Kennedy Center, Seattle Children's Theatre, Louisville's Stage One, Arizona's Childsplay, the Smithsonian, the California Theatre Center and at international festivals in Canada, Sweden, Japan, Scotland, Germany and France. She lives in Washington, D.C. with actor/designer Kevin Reese and their daughter, Malinda.